# Curves in Motion

DETAIL OF FANTASY FORM #1634

# Curves in Motion

## Quilt Designs & Techniques

### Judy B. Dales

Editor: Annie Nelson
Technical Editor: Joyce Engels Lytle
Book Design: Ewa Gavrielov © 1998 C&T Publishing
Cover Production: John Cram
Cover Design: Kathy Lee
Graphic Illustrations: Christina Jarumay, Alan McCorkle, and
Jay Richards © 1998 C&T Publishing
Front Cover Image: Detail of *Dancing on the Dark Side of the
Moon*, 1997, 42" x 59", Judy B. Dales. Photo: Carina Woolrich
© 1998 C&T Publishing
Back Cover Image: *Nightfall In the Desert*, 1997, 50" x 50",
Judy B. Dales
Photography: Karen Bell unless otherwise noted

**Library of Congress Cataloging-in-Publication Data**
Dales, Judy B.
    Curves in motion: quilt designs & techniques /
    Judy B. Dales
        p.        cm.
    Includes bibliographical references and index.
    ISBN 1-57120-052-5 (PBK.)
    1. Patchwork.    2. Quilting.    3. Curves.
    I. Title.
    TT835.D34        1998
    746.46'041--DC21        98-15529
                    CIP

Published by C&T Publishing, Inc.
P.O. Box 1456
Lafayette, California 94549

Printed in Hong Kong
10    9    8    7    6    5    4    3

# Table of Contents

# Dedication

*To my husband, Andy, who enables, encourages, and applauds, even though he may not always completely understand the forces that drive me.*

*To my mother, Narcissa Cameron Boyd, who was always so proud of my accomplishments and would have been thrilled with this book.*

*To my father, William Boyd, who encouraged me to begin this book and shared the stress of writing it, but did not live to see its completion.*

# Acknowledgments

A special thanks goes to Joyce Lytle, who made the right phone call at the wrong time, and then persevered to make it again at the right time. This book would never have become reality if it hadn't been for her encouragement at the opportune moment. Thanks also to all those who have pushed, prodded and, yes, nagged this most reluctant author, chief among them "the assistant with attitude," Bonnie Adams. Without your input, I might still be just thinking about it!

I am grateful to all the quiltmakers who have so generously shared their quilts: Peggy Stocks, Mary Nehring, Deb Lybarger, Jodee Todd, Pat Crucil, Lisa Sharpe, Mary Smith, Priscilla Hair, Vicki Ibison, Mildred Dort, and Lois Griffin. Thank you!

Special thanks to Kim Ritter, Darcy Young, and Laurie Martecchini for testing the techniques and patterns, and for the lovely quilts that are the result.

Many thanks to Amy Helfrick, who has proofread practically everything I have ever written, including the first draft of this manuscript, and now knows more about curved seam piecing than she ever wanted to know!

I am especially indebted to Karen Bell, who not only traveled halfway across the country to do the photography for this book, but also collected, organized, tidied, photographed, repacked, and shipped most of the quilts included here. Her hard work, experience, professionalism, and attention to detail were invaluable and very much appreciated.

Thanks to all the folks at C&T Publishing for guiding me through this process: Annie Nelson, my editor; Joyce Lytle, who checked every curve and had the courage to let me loose with color; Jay Richards, who pulled me through more than one technical crisis; Diane Pedersen, for her continual guidance, and all the other people who have worked so hard on this book.

Also, thank you to each and every student who encouraged the writing of this book and the friends who have suffered through its creation. The creative interaction that takes place in the classroom, and at meetings, whenever quilters gather together, is a great motivational force, and this book is a product of that creative exchange. Many of the ideas and concepts are my own creation, but many more are the result of other quilters sharing their knowledge and experience. This effort is just a small part of the long tradition of sharing that is so integral to the quilting tradition, and this book is my way of returning to the quilt world the gifts other quilters have shared with me over the years.

# Preface

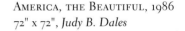
AMERICA, THE BEAUTIFUL, 1986
72" x 72", *Judy B. Dales*

This quilt was the New Jersey winner in the Statue of Liberty Quilt Contest, which was sponsored by The Museum of American Folk Art in New York City to celebrate the Centennial of the statue. Collection of the *Newark Museum*, Newark, NJ. Photo: *Myron Miller*

My first free-form curved design was *America, the Beautiful*, made for the Statue of Liberty Quilt Contest, and I will never know where I found the courage to begin this project. I knew nothing about working with curves, but I was burning with enthusiasm and began the project, blissfully unaware of just how ignorant I was!

The contest theme of celebration, patriotism, and freedom held strong appeal to me, and the song "America, the Beautiful" by Katherine Lee Bates and Samuel A. Ward has always been one of my favorites, so I chose the phrases from this song to be the basis of my design. The purple mountains, fruited plains, and spacious skies were easy to depict, but I had real difficulty with "amber waves of grain." The notion of slender grain stalks topped with rounded tufts filled me with trepidation. I could just see myself appliquéing little grain doodads till the wee hours every night. That thought was horrifying enough to keep me in the procrastination mode for several months.

I had almost decided to abandon the whole project when I stumbled across a greeting card with a beautiful Oriental design of amber and gold. When I realized that the design was actually waves, I had the solution to my problem. I could depict amber waves, which would be enough to suggest grain, thus cleverly avoiding all the hours of tedious appliqué!

The process of making this particular quilt was stressful, educational, and exhilarating. I learned very quickly why it is essential to make a tracing of your master pattern, rather than cutting up the original. If the original is dissected to use as templates, there is nothing to guide you in putting the pieces back together, and the assembly of the quilt becomes a jigsaw puzzle challenge. I didn't know about registration and intersection marks, so each curved seam was a wild adventure. I used decorator weight fabrics for the first time, because the colors and printed patterns expressed my theme so well. Whether I could actually piece them together and hand quilt them remained a huge question mark throughout the major part of the process.

On the positive side of the equation was the excitement generated when I saw the design coming together. The first section up on the design wall was the "amber waves," and I was thrilled by the flowing lines of the curves and sensuous rhythm of the waves. I knew I was onto something pretty spectacular when my older son, who was about fifteen at the time, happened to be passing by, stopped dead in his tracks, and exclaimed "Wow!"

The quilt was finished in a little over two months, sent to New York for the contest, and designated the New Jersey winner. Immediately after the contest, The Newark Museum purchased the quilt, which provided a very happy ending for this quilt after all the chaos and stress associated with its creation.

I view this quilt as one of the most significant I have ever produced, because it marks the beginning of my romance with curves. The success of my initial encounter with free-form curves convinced me that they are well worth the extra effort required. I love the soft, feminine quality a curved line brings to a design, and the fact that incorporating curves into my work allows a more faithful reproduction of the world around me.

AMERICA THE BEAUTIFUL, work in progress

Chapter One
# Introduction

DANCING ON THE DARK SIDE OF THE MOON, 1997
42" x 59", *Judy B. Dales*

This is the third in a series of Fantasy Form quilts. The main shapes
are pieced, but tulle and transparent chiffon have been applied to the
background areas to create a watercolor effect. The quilt is machine
pieced, appliquéd, and quilted. Photo: *Carina Woolrich*

# The Path of Discovery
## Patterns with the Illusion of a Curve

Like most quilters, I started with straight-seam designs
when I began to quilt, because very few of the
traditional curve-seam blocks, such as Drunkard's
Path or Snowball, appealed to me. However, I have
always been drawn to patterns with curves, those
with a circular theme, or straight-seam designs that
produce the illusion of a curve, such as Storm at
Sea and Kaleidoscope. The illusory curve in these
designs is produced by using contrasts to accentuate
the diagonal seam in the corner of the blocks.

THE PENTAGON, 1983
96" x 90, *Judy B. Dales.* Photo: *Marion Conners and Clarice
Marie Burch*

SERENITY, 1979
37" x 37", *Judy B. Dales*

In this small wallhanging, there is the strong illusion of a circle,
but in actuality, all seams are straight. Photo: *Judy B. Dales*

## Geometry As a Bridge

I have worked for years with Islamic patterns, which
are found throughout the Mediterranean area and are
usually worked in tile, marble, and wood. These deco-
rative patterns are based on a circle and are drafted
using only a compass and a straight edge. The resulting
designs are often very circular, either containing
a ring of stars around a large central star, or utilizing
actual curves in various parts of the design.

PALE REFLECTIONS, 1986
56" x 56", *Judy B. Dales.* Photo: *Marion Conners and Clarice
Marie Burch*

I realize now that there were many different influences leading to my involvement with curves, and one of the strongest was my love of geometry and the compass. Although I hated math in school and struggled through every math course I took, I put geometry in a totally different category. In my opinion, geometry has less to do with numbers (which are my downfall), and much more to do with logical thinking and visual perception.

I remember spending many happy hours in high school doodling with a compass, and it was in fact a compass doodle that brought me to curved-seam patchwork many years later. I had taken a class in which we used a compass to draw a series of concentric rings within a square, and the class project was a very small quilt based on that one block. When I got home, I played around with my compass, using it to create a few small-scale designs with circles and curves. Those designs may never have gone any further had I not, just at that time, discovered the yardstick compass, which enabled me to draft the patterns full-scale, removing the major stumbling block that previously had prevented the small-sized compass doodles from becoming quilt designs.

I immediately started to scale up some of my compass drawings to full size quilt patterns, and *Circle Study* is one of the resulting quilts. I was a little hesitant about working with all those curves, but quickly discovered that accuracy and careful sewing enabled me to produce a pieced top that lay perfectly flat.

CIRCLE STUDY, 1985
52" x 52", *Judy B. Dales*

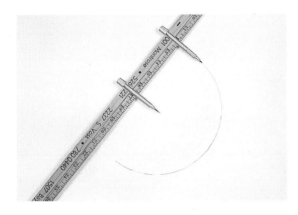

A yardstick compass is an ingenious little tool that turns any long, thin ruler or piece of wood into a large compass. Griffin Manufacturing Company makes one that I use and like very much.

## Appliqué Avoidance

Another factor that greatly encouraged my discovery of curved-seam piecing was my dislike of appliqué. I greatly admire appliquéd quilts and their unique designs, but have decided that I personally don't want to make any of them! *Growing Up at the Lodge* is one of my very few appliquéd quilts. Notice what a unique and effective backdrop the pieced curves provide for the appliquéd vignettes. This quilt was the New Jersey runner-up in the Memories of Childhood Contest at The Great American Quilt Festival, and it depicts scenes from my childhood growing up in northern Vermont. I think it is very appropriate that the quilt belongs to my cousins, David and Wilhelmina Smith, who now own the Highland Lodge (my childhood home). When I requested their permission to use an image of the Lodge in the quilt, David didn't hesitate for a second. He graciously gave permission, but requested that I include the phone number to call for reservations. I happily obliged!

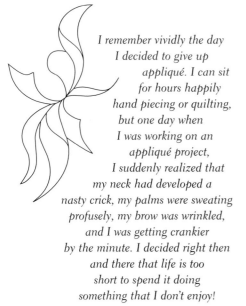

*I remember vividly the day I decided to give up appliqué. I can sit for hours happily hand piecing or quilting, but one day when I was working on an appliqué project, I suddenly realized that my neck had developed a nasty crick, my palms were sweating profusely, my brow was wrinkled, and I was getting crankier by the minute. I decided right then and there that life is too short to spend it doing something that I don't enjoy!*

GROWING UP AT THE LODGE, 1988
54" x 45", *Judy B. Dales*. Collection of the *Highland Lodge*.
Photo: *Young Masters Studio*

DETAIL OF GROWING UP AT THE LODGE

Traditionally, if you wished to create a representational design, the appliqué technique was used rather than piecework. Pictorial and realistic images were usually created by stitching an appropriately-shaped piece of fabric onto a background fabric. The curved portions presented no more of a problem than other parts of the design, because the edges were simply turned under with the needle and stitched down, similar to straight areas.

Since I had vowed to no longer subject myself to the agony of appliqué, it was natural for me to develop an alternative method of creating pictorial and representational designs using piecing instead. I quickly discovered that although these types of designs can be created using geometric shapes, the addition of curves produces a much more realistic effect.

## Curves Within a Grid

The first curved piecing method I experimented with was Joyce Schlotzhauer's Two Patch Curve System. The basic unit is similar to a Drunkard's Path block where a curved seam divides a square into two patches. However, Joyce made the curve a little more gentle so that it would be easier to piece, and brought the end of the seam to the actual corners of the square to improve the continuity of line when multiple squares were joined.

Joyce's three books on the subject offered unlimited design inspiration, and in the third book she altered the scale of the square grid to produce variations in the curve. *February Fantasy* was made for Joyce's second book, *Curves Unlimited*, which featured abstract two patch curve designs. The quilt was also featured on the cover of *Quilter's Newsletter Magazine*, February, 1985.

FEBRUARY FANTASY, 1984
75" x 75", *Judy B. Dales.* Collection of *Nancy Jo Drum.*
Photo: *Marion Conners and Clarice Marie Burch*

## Breaking Out of the Grid

While I enjoyed the two patch curve design system, it wasn't long before I began to find working within a square grid extremely confining. Changing the scale of the grid in order to change the size and sharpness of the curve seemed extremely tedious, and I finally decided it would just be easier to draw the curves freehand.

## Advantages of Working with Curves

### Freedom with Curves

I discovered that there is great freedom in designing with curves. The precision associated with geometric design is not a factor when working with curves; an angle can be any size, and a line can bend as sharply or smoothly as you wish. In fact, a line need not be strongly curved to be effective. Sometimes a gentle curve is more elegant and appealing than a sharp one, and it is certainly easier to piece! Long skinny points, which can look so intimidating, can dwindle to a whisper and be no harder to manage technically than any other seams. Perfect points are one of the most amazing advantages of piecing a curved design and happen rather effortlessly with careful marking and accurate sewing.

One of the more freeing aspects of designing with curves is the fact that there is no such thing as a "right" or "wrong" curve. A curve need only be graceful to be effective, and learning exactly where a curve should be placed is largely a matter of experimentation. Although curved designs can be representational, abstract designs are equally as effective. Knowing that a design doesn't have to be realistic, or to depict recognizable images, is a very freeing notion.

Although I still like geometric designs, discovering curves has changed my quilts and my life. I feel as if I have been set free—free from the restrictions of precise angles, minute measurements, and drafting accuracy. Working with curves has opened up a world of immense beauty, excitement, and grace. I hope that my enthusiasm for curves will inspire you to also explore the world of curves.

Tears; A Healing Quilt, 1992
55" x 72", *Judy B. Dales*

This quilt was the fourth in a series of abstract curved designs, and the first piece I did
after my mother died. It took almost six months after my mother's death to begin any new
work, and during the design process, the curves became tears. The making of this quilt
was very therapeutic and marked the return of the creative spirit after a long, dark spell.
Photo: *The Photographic House, Inc.*

Chapter Two
# Designing with Curves

The Rose, 1991
48" x 62", *Judy B. Dales*

The glorious seed catalogs that flood the mailbox every year are
enough to inspire any number of quilts.

# Preparation

## Get Into the Mood

As you begin to tune into curves, you will discover lovely design sources everywhere. When you begin to search for curves in your environment, you may find yourself becoming enamored of some of them, as I did. My obsession with round things led me to start collecting marbles, antique glass floats, and anything with grape motifs.

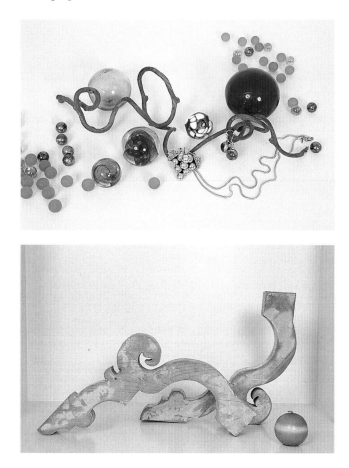

My husband thought I was crazy when I brought home two pieces of "gingerbread" after an antiquing expedition, but I fell in love with the curves. I have collected many books with photographs of waves, clouds, birds, and other curved forms. Learning how to draw and piece curves has expanded my design horizons, and I no longer eliminate a particular design because it seems too difficult or inappropriate for patchwork. I know that I can use curves to capture the essence of any image, and I am also confident that anything that can be drawn on a piece of paper can be cut apart and reassembled in fabric to create a quilt top.

Before working with curves, it helps if you prepare yourself emotionally and mentally. Listen to soft, mellow music to get you in the mood. Feel how the music flows and picture the curved melodic line. Close your eyes and run your fingers over a curved piece of sculpture. Hold a large marble in your hand and appreciate its roundness.

I find that I am attracted to anything with a curvilinear form, such as the objects below. The special properties of glass seem to accentuate the appeal of rounded shapes and forms.

Study the curved lines of a chandelier, a vase, a flower. Try to saturate your mind's eye with the sense of roundness; let your soul be seduced by the beauty of curves. Then when it is time to sit down and put pencil to paper, the essence of curves will already be a part of you and will flow naturally from your hand.

## Practice Makes Perfect

You will find that the more you work with curves, the easier it becomes and the more natural it feels. When you begin drawing curves, you will probably feel timid, and you may be discouraged with your first efforts. I urge you to persevere! The more curves you draw, the easier it will be, the more natural it will feel, and I promise that you will get better with practice. As you become more familiar with curves, you will become more comfortable with them, which allows you to be more expansive and free flowing with your designs. I keep all my drawings, regardless of whether they are suitable for quilt designs. I will often come back to an older design and rework it.

When I teach a class on curves, the students are amazed at the way I can alter a line very slightly to make a curve look dramatically better. This is not due to great talent on my part. It is simply that I have worked with curves for a long time, and through experimentation and practice, I have learned what looks best. Many times I will try two or three different curves before I find the one that is the most graceful or suitable for that design. This is normal and natural. And this is why erasers were created! Sketching is a process that all artists employ. Lightly draw two, three, or four lines, then choose the one that is best. Editing is easier than writing from scratch. Choosing the best line from several lightly sketched lines is much easier than drawing one perfectly the first time!

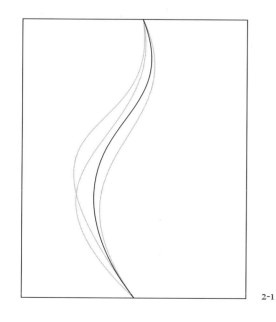

2-1

## Creativity Enhancement

When you are designing it is important to stay in a carefree and adventurous mood. Sometimes it helps to pretend that you are a six-year-old. Remember how fun it used to be to draw and color, and how pleased you usually were with your efforts? Try to shuck off the many layers of anxiety and disappointment concerning artistic endeavors that you have acquired in the intervening years. Start out with the idea that this is fun—and it *should* be fun! Try to be relaxed and have a good time.

Don't expect your first efforts to be wonderful. You are beginning a new process and learning a new skill, so you can't assume that you will do well on your first try. You will improve as you go along, but if your expectations are too great to start with, you are setting yourself up for failure.

Choose a time to try the design exercises when you will not be interrupted, if possible. Eliminate distractions and allow yourself more than one session. Learning new techniques and design approaches takes time and won't be accomplished in one day. Sometimes new ideas need to sink into your subconscious for a while before they really begin to make sense.

Try to put all technical worries and considerations aside when you are drawing. Worrying about the tightness of a curve, seam intersections, skinny points, and other sewing problems will only cause you to freeze up and lose your sense of adventure. These problems can be addressed, and corrected, at a later stage of the quiltmaking process. For now, they only interfere with the flow of creativity. Concentrate on making the design look the way you want it to, and assure yourself that alterations can be made later that will not significantly change the design, but will make it technically possible.

## Be Kind to Yourself

It is important not to give up on a design too soon. Chances are, the first few lines won't look like much, but that's normal. A design really needs to reach a certain point before it can be evaluated. Judging your efforts too early in the design process is inappropriate and counter-productive, but it is something that we all tend to do. Negative phrases such as "This is really ugly," "I can't do this," or "I'm not very creative," rebound around in our heads and inhibit creativity.

It is almost as if there is a little judgmental person inside us who is super critical, and constantly ridicules our efforts. This little person actually has an important function in real life, which is to warn us of danger and help us make decisions that keep us safe. It is often essential to heed those warnings if we are to survive. However, when you are trying to be creative, it is important to ignore all those annoying warnings. Avoid being inhibited by fears of failure. Tell your little judgmental person to go sit in the corner while you work. Assure him that he will be recalled at a later time, when it is appropriate to evaluate your work. Keep him quiet for now so that you can work without inhibitions and worry, and capture a spirit of playfulness and adventure.

## Dealing with Anxiety

Fear of failure is one of the most harmful emotions for any quiltmaker because it can bring total paralysis. It is essential to accept failure as being an integral part of the creative process. If you want to make progress, both technically and artistically, you must be willing to experiment, to take risks, and when you take risks, it is inevitable that you will fail some of the time. In fact, if you don't fail sometimes, perhaps it is a signal that you are not pushing yourself hard enough. If you remember that failure is simply a part of the learning process, you can put it in the proper perspective and then, hopefully, it will no longer impede your creativity.

David Bayles and Ted Orland have written a wonderful book on the subject of creativity, called *Art and Fear, Observations on the Perils (and Rewards) of Artmaking.* The basic premise is that making art is not a magical process available to only a few. Rather, it is something that everyone can do. Creating art is simply a matter of making enough work (whether that work is painting, writing, quilting, etc.), and working hard enough and long enough at it that a percentage of what is produced will be worthy of the title "Art." Sounds rather simplistic, but it is basically the old theory of practice makes perfect. Their advice to anyone involved in making art is to just keep on creating whatever it is that you create, and they provide wonderful suggestions as to how to manage to do just that. I highly recommend this book. It is very down to earth and has wonderful thoughts for people who want to be more creative.

## Getting Started

It is always helpful to have all the tools you need when you begin a project. I have discovered that not only do the proper tools make all parts of the sewing process easier, but having the proper materials for designing can enhance your creativity. I find a large stack of smooth, white paper very stimulating, and I have discovered that the stack needs to be big enough that I feel I can afford a few false starts. Nothing is more inhibiting than having only one piece of paper!

I also recommend the use of tracing paper overlays, which can greatly enhance creativity. Sometimes we find ourselves paralyzed and unable to continue with a design because we are afraid that any changes will ruin it, not make it better. Using layers of tracing paper in the course of creating a design allows you to alter the design innumerable times without losing the parts that are satisfactory. If you don't like the way your drawing is progressing, simply replace the tracing paper and start again. Trace the parts you like and drop out the parts that aren't working. Knowing that you won't lose the good parts can be very reassuring, and may help you be a bit more adventurous. I often do fifteen or twenty tracings to produce one drawing!

## Adding Curves
## to Straight-line Blocks
### Straight Lines to Curves

It is a good idea to approach the design process gradually, and that is what we will do here. Replacing straight lines in traditional blocks is not a difficult maneuver, but it will dramatically alter the look of the block. This exercise will give you an appreciation for the impact of curves and allow you to work with curves within a structured environment. This is not a difficult exercise, so don't make it hard! Don't expect to create a free-form abstract design from this project. That will come later. For now, just see how different a block can look if you curve off some of the lines.

You can use the blocks I have provided in the illustration on page 21, or any other blocks, traditional or your original designs. Tracing or photocopying the blocks onto a piece of paper might be easier than working in the book, but be sure to work with a tracing paper overlay. Don't tape the tracing paper down, as you may want to shift the paper in order to work with a block more than once. Draw the outer boundaries of the block on the tracing paper, though it is not necessary to retrace the whole block. You should be able to see it clearly through the tracing paper. At any stage, you can lift up the tracing paper, which will cause the lines of the original block to drop out, thus allowing you to see how your design is progressing. Any lines that you decide should remain straight lines should be redrawn on your tracing paper.

*I learned the importance
of tracing paper the hard way.
I had created an original
block design that
I had meticulously redrawn
again and again to form a repeat
pattern. When I began to try different
colorations of the pattern, I made
a mistake and colored something
wrong. If I had been working on
an overlay, I could have just
discarded the paper
with the mistake and started with a fresh sheet.
Unfortunately, the unalterable mistake on the
original drawing dampened my enthusiasm for the
project to such a degree that progress stopped right
there. Tracing paper would have
allowed a second try!*

Try to find a workplace where you will have good light, a comfortable chair, and uncluttered space. I use a mechanical pencil with a 0.7mm lead for drawing, but any pencil will be fine as long as it glides smoothly and freely on the paper and makes a mark that is clearly visible. Some of the mechanical pencils have very hard, thin lead that digs into the paper rather than gliding. With curves, you need to be able to move freely. Be sure to have a good eraser. A fine-tip marker is helpful if you want to draw the lines in darker and more permanently.

UNEXPECTED RESULTS, 1997
43" x 43", *Judy B. Dales*

This quilt is based on the block in the middle of the top row of the first design exercise shown on the opposite page. The block is not completely symmetrical, so it worked best rotated around the center point. The border was a complete experiment and provides a perfect example of a good idea that didn't work quite right the first time. I can't decide whether it is the strong print or the curved seam that is causing the borders to overwhelm the block design, but I will definitely try the curved border treatment again.

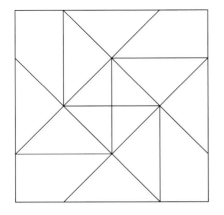
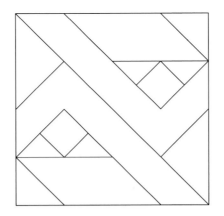
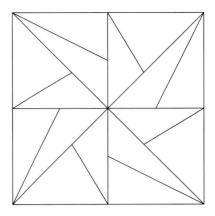

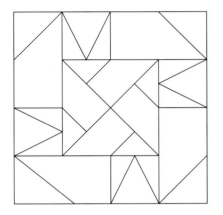
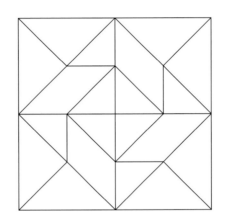
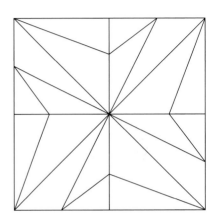

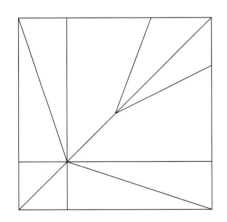
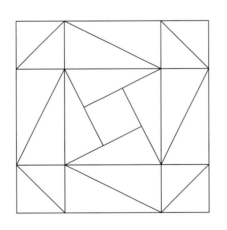
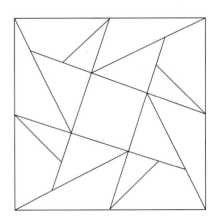

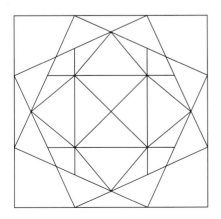
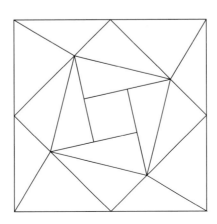
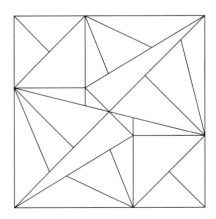

As you gain experience with this design approach, allow your curves to extend longer distances, but work initially on only a single segment of a line (for example, the line between points A and B in the illustration below). Later on, you can be a little more adventurous.

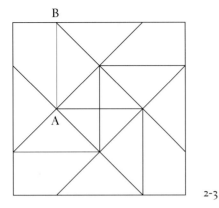

2-3

When you replace a straight line with a curve, you have the choice of putting the curve on either side of the line, and it is necessary to experiment in order to discover which yields the most interesting result.

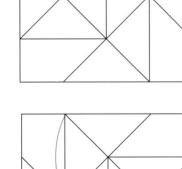

2-4A

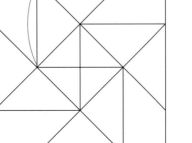

2-4B

You can also draw an S-curve that bends first one way, then the other. This produces a very graceful effect, but sewing it will require a bit more effort.

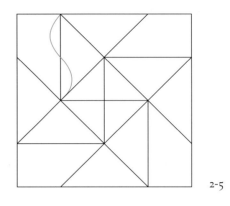

2-5

You might put a curve on both sides of the line simultaneously, which creates a leaf shape. Occasionally a design will call for such a shape, but most of the time, it should be avoided. Keep the curves gentle—they don't need to be sharp or deep to be effective.

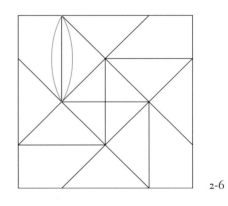

2-6

This may be the first time in many years that you have drawn a curve, and you may feel quite awkward. Don't be concerned with the aesthetic qualities of the curves at this point, just do the best you can. Keep the curves fairly gentle, and don't get upset if they don't turn out just the way you want.

## Working Symmetrically or Asymmetrically

If the block you are working with is symmetrical, the four quadrants will be the same. Therefore, if you replace a line in one quadrant, you should replace it in the other three. The only difficult thing about this is that the curve should go in the same direction in each quadrant, but as you move to the various quadrants, it will appear as if the line is going in the opposite direction. This is because the quadrants rotate around the center of the block. If you have trouble with this part of the process, talk yourself through it. For example, "I made this line bend in toward the middle,"…etc. If that doesn't help, simply rotate your paper a quarter of a turn, and draw the line exactly the same each time.

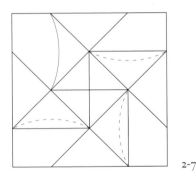

2-7

When you start adding curves to your block, you won't know how the design will end up and that's all right. You are not supposed to know. Start by adding one line in the first quadrant, then reproduce that same line in the other three quadrants, as in 2-8A. Draw your second line in each quadrant (2-8B) and then the third line (2-8C). Continue in this manner until you've finished, run out of space and options, or you think the design is complete, whichever comes first! Notice that I was uncertain as to how to finish the center of this block, so I experimented with several different options.

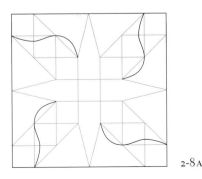

2-8A

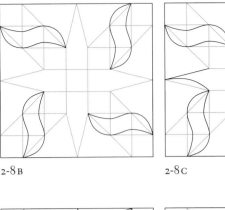

2-8B                    2-8C

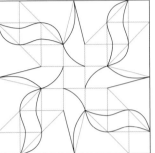

2-8D                    2-8E

2-8F                    2-8G

Remember that the original straight-line block is there purely to help you get started. If at any point it ceases to be beneficial and becomes distracting, simply remove it from underneath the tracing paper and continue with your own design. Also, feel free to ignore, eliminate, or change any lines in the original block that don't appeal to you. Remember that during the design process you are in charge, so feel free to make any changes you deem appropriate.

Be sure that each curved line you add connects to another line. If it doesn't, the result will be a design that cannot be pieced because the unconnected lines do not form complete shapes. The lines in 2-9A create a charming design, but one that cannot be pieced. Several of the lines need to be extended so that they connect with another line and form a complete shape, as has been done in 2-9B. Occasionally, the curved lines need to extend further than the straight lines that inspired them.

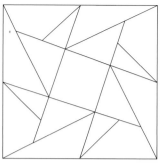

2-10 A

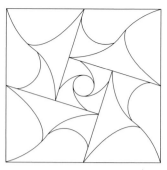

2-10 B

2-9 A

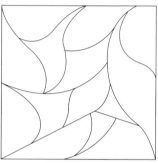

2-10 C

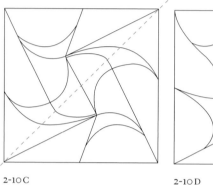

2-10 D

2-9 B

The asymmetrical block can form a symmetrical design when four blocks are rotated around a central point, as in 2-10E.

There may be times when you don't want the finished curved block to be perfectly symmetrical, and in that case, you simply figure out which way you want the lines to go and be systematic about it. The design created from the block in 2-10A can be perfectly symmetrical (2-10B), partially symmetrical (the two diagonal halves of 2-10C are identical, but one needs to be rotated to match the other), or completely asymmetrical (2-10D).

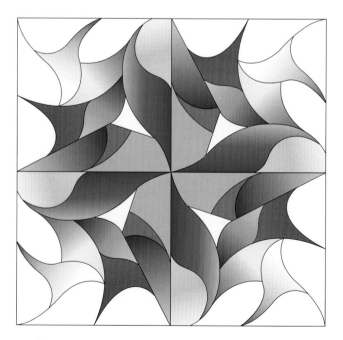

2-10 E

## Straight Versus Curved Lines

Sometimes it is best to leave a few straight lines in your block. The single curve in 2-11 B seems more effective than the three employed in 2-11 A. The contrast between straight lines and curves can be charming, and one beautiful curve can go a long way.

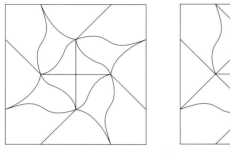

2-11 A            2-11 B

If there are too many curves, the result can be somewhat overwhelming. In fact, if you get completely carried away, you could end up with a design that looks like snowballs, which is not the least bit attractive. It is not uncommon to find that you have suddenly added a few too many curves. Luckily a fresh piece of tracing paper provides a new start! You will quickly get a feel for the proper balance between straight and curved lines.

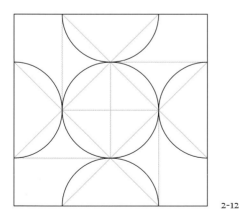

2-12

Keep in mind that simple designs are often the most effective. One beautifully placed line can be far more effective than three or four which break the surface into too many small pieces. Not only are a lot of small pieces daunting to the person who will eventually sew the block (!), but they can create a visually cluttered look.

At this point in the design process, concentrate on creating a pleasing block. Don't worry about how many points are intersecting in the middle, how many pieces will need to be sewn, or how several blocks will join together. Just concentrate on one, single block, and save those other considerations for later.

*I personally have a great deal of trouble knowing when to stop. I tend to keep adding lines and pieces until I have created a monster, at which point I have to mentally slap myself and start chanting, "Keep it simple!" I have finally come to realize that my tendency to overwork designs is a definite liability, and I now try hard to keep that impulse under control.*

NIGHTFALL IN THE DESERT, 1997
50" x 50", *Judy B. Dales*

The curves in this original block create a swirling feeling
of movement, yet are not difficult to piece.

## Original Block Designs
### Create a Block

After drawing blocks on top of a patchwork grid, the
next logical step is to create an original block without
the help of a grid. Draw several blank squares on
graph paper and cover with a tracing paper overlay.

I like to work with a fairly large block, as I find that a
small block can interfere with the flow and rhythm of
the curves. Try a three or four inch block to see if that
is a comfortable size for you. You may find it helpful
to do some free-form drawing exercises, as described
in this chapter starting on page 48, before you begin,
to help loosen up both your arm and your brain.

Your original blocks can be all curved seams or a combination of curved and straight seams. Begin by putting three lines in a block. If you are very lucky, you may find that three lines is all you need. If not, keep adding lines and experimenting until you have a pleasing block.

## Enjoy the Freedom

In the beginning, you may feel intimidated by the lack of structure. There is no grid to work on, and the square is not divided into segments as with straight-line patchwork blocks. Rather than feeling inhibited by this, allow it to set you free! Start a line any old place on the edge of the block, let it wander to exactly where it wants to go, and allow intersections to fall where they will. Once you get used to the freedom, you will love it!

## Think Positively

As you begin creating blocks, remember not to be too critical of your efforts. It is not unusual to draw ten or fifteen blocks in order to produce one that is usable. Don't think of the discarded ones as failures; think of them as stepping stones that moved you along to the one successful block. Keep in mind, also, that a block that looks quite uninspiring when it is all alone, can be fabulous in multiple formation. For example, this design with only five lines and six pieces does not look very interesting on its own, but creates a charming design when repeated and rotated. Don't judge a block too harshly until you have fully explored its potential.

However, at this point it is best to work with a single block. Even though it is important to be aware of the potential for secondary designs, I feel that working with more than one block at this stage can be confusing. Occasionally, if I work with multiples, I will be seduced by a wonderful secondary design and get carried away with it, only to find that parts of my original block have suffered from lack of attention. When I work with only one block, concentrating on making it look as balanced and interesting as possible, I can then be pleasantly surprised when I see what lovely things happen when four blocks are combined. However, try working both ways, either with a single block or multiples, and decide which works best for you.

When you have a block that pleases you, there are a number of things to check before you move on to the next step. The first decision is how you want to use the block. If it is a very intricate design, such as those shown in the photos on pages 31 and 54, and on page 123, it could be drafted quite large and one block used for a wallhanging, in which case several interesting borders would finish it off nicely. On the other hand, if the block design is quite simple, multiples could be used in the standard 12" size or any appropriate block size. The photo on the opposite page shows a design used as a repeat block. Chapter Three (pages 62 to 78) discusses the technical problems that need to be identified and corrected, how to decide on a finished size, how to enlarge your design, how to evaluate the curves from both a technical and artistic standpoint, and other refinements. Read that section before moving on to the next step.

2-13 A

2-13 B

IN THE WIND, 1997
66" x 87", *Judy B. Dales*

Although it doesn't look it, this quilt is based on a repeated block. The
actual block is kite shaped, but it is the secondary patterns and the blurred
block definition that make this design so fascinating.

# Combining Blocks
## Working with Multiples

If you have decided to use multiples of your block, you will need to experiment with different combinations to see which yields the most interesting design. Trace or copy your block so that you have eight duplicates, which will enable you to try all the different combinations. You might also wish to trace or copy the design so that you have a reversed block, which often yields interesting results. It is not uncommon to discover realistic images with mirrored (reversed) blocks, such as the owl face in 2-14 B or the hearts and ribbons design in 2-14 D.

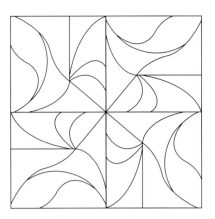

2-15 A

2-14 A

2-14 B

2-14 C

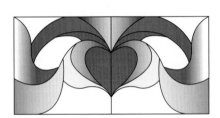

2-14 D

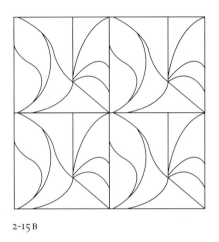

2-15 B

## Different Symmetries

When you start experimenting with your blocks and have trouble figuring out which way your blocks should go, put a different colored dot in each corner. Then match up the same colors when you rotate, to get the proper combination. Ruth McDowell's book *Symmetry* explains all the different ways to rotate, flip, and repeat a block, and each of the different arrangements is worth trying at least once. In addition to the combinations that are typical of quilt blocks, Ruth introduces some that you may not have thought to try that yield very interesting results. These are just a few of the possible combinations.

You will discover that not all combinations look good for any given block, so it is important to try a variety of combinations before you reject a block. If the block formation doesn't produce a flowing design, the purpose of working with curves has been defeated, so you may have to make some changes to produce a design with a lot of swirl and movement.

## Editing the Results

As you see the interesting secondary patterns forming, you may wish to add, eliminate, or change a line to emphasize an interesting shape or line. Great care needs to be taken to find a line with just the right curve, paying particular attention to the shapes formed on either side of the line. Often the one that turns out to be right is the one you least expected.

Several different lines were added to the large petal shape in the center of the four blocks in 2-16A, in an attempt to decrease its size. The line added in 2-16B and C did little to enhance the flow of the curves. In fact, the new shapes that were formed distract the eye from the lovely curves in the rest of the block. The line added to 2-16D performed the intended function a little better, but I decided finally to leave the large petal shape intact. While it definitely draws attention, the eye moves along its strong curve and continues outward to explore other parts of the block. In 2-16E, a line added in a completely different place has an unexpected effect. It curves in the opposite direction from the other lines, and acts to counter balance the predominant flow to make the block more interesting.

Occasionally, you may encounter a situation where you need to alter a few lines, so that the blocks join more gracefully. Lines do not always have to meet at block boundaries, but if they come close, they should actually meet, or be changed enough that they don't look like a near miss. Also, be watching for two edge shapes that combine to create a larger, unattractive shape. An additional line may be needed to break up that awkward shape.

2-16A

2-16B

2-16C

2-16D

2-16E

Fantasy Form #101, 1997
44" x 43", *Judy B. Dales*

Even though this design has a free-form flair to it, it is actually
a result of the multi-block design exercise. The underlying grid
is symmetrical and organized, but the resulting curved design
need not be.

# Adding Curves to Multi-block Designs
## Change of Space

I have discovered that some quilters really enjoy working with a single block, but other folks feel restricted by
the limited working space a single block provides. Some
people prefer more space and more freedom. If you were
disappointed with your efforts with the single blocks, you
may discover that this exercise appeals to you more. On
the other hand, you may have been very happy working
with a single block, and this exercise may terrify you.
Don't be intimidated! There are a lot of lines in these
designs, but you don't have to use all of them!!

2-17
I call this original block design "Cubic Star." Because it is repeated four times, you can create a completely symmetrical design, but you don't have to, of course.

2-18
This design was formed using the same block four times. Notice
that the corners of the blocks that come to the center have been
altered to provide more interest in the center of the design.

The procedure for this exercise is basically the
same as the previous one, but you have more space
in which to work and a lot more lines to choose from,
all of which gives you more options. If there are four
blocks in each design, you can create a symmetrical
design by repeating each step in all four quadrants.
However, you may choose to try an asymmetrical
design, and both the four-block units and the six-block
units are suitable for asymmetry.

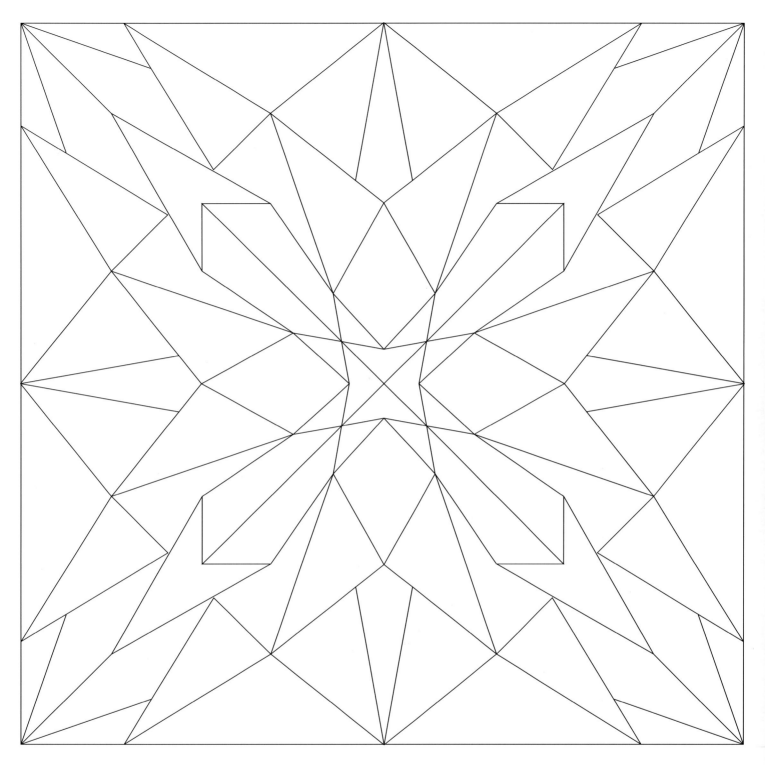

2-20
This design is medallion style, but that doesn't necessarily
mean that the curve design you create must be also.

2-19 (Opposite page)
Six blocks are combined to provide a rectangular format,
but you could choose to use only four of them.

Because the underlying design is larger and more complex, it is not necessary to follow the geometric design as closely as we did in the last exercise. In fact, I encourage you to be freer with your lines and curves. Don't let the geometric design restrict or intimidate you. Remember that you can ignore or change lines, extend lines past major intersections, or remove the original design completely. These two curved designs were both created from the geometric diagram on the previous page. Figure 2-21A follows the underlying structure fairly closely, which resulted in a symmetrical design, but Figure 2-21B is much more relaxed and asymmetrical. Notice that only the intersection points in the grid were actually used in B, but having the grid structure to work with provides a place to start and specific points where a line can begin and end.

2-21A

## Tracing Paper Tricks

If you find that you have created a wonderful design in the center portion of the block, but are baffled by how to finish the outer parts, use a second tracing-paper overlay, which will enable you to work the different sections without interfering with the part you've already done. You can experiment with several different options and then choose the one that works best. If, however, nothing seems to work, consider making your block just a little smaller!

Another little trick I use is to repeat a portion of the design that I find particularly appealing. If you trace this onto a separate piece of paper, it can be slipped under the overlay and positioned in different ways to repeat the segment in various places in the design. Repetition of this kind can be very effective.

2-21B

## Evaluate the Results

When you have a design you like, it needs to be evaluated in the same way the single blocks were. Obviously, if your design is very complex, you will need to enlarge it significantly to allow for all the pieces. On the other hand, you may have created quite a simple block in spite of all the lines you started with, in which case, you would probably make it a standard size, 10" or 12", and use it as a repeat block. Don't allow the original design inspiration to dictate what you do with the finished product. That decision is made based purely on the results. The design shown here emerged from the six-block grid, but is much less complex than the underlying structure. Although each block in the original grid would need to be at least 12" to be a manageable sewing size (meaning the whole grid would measure 24" x 36"), an appropriate size for the resulting curved design would probably be no more than 18" x 27". When you have decided on an appropriate size, the design can be enlarged by drafting the underlying geometric blocks up to the appropriate size and then redrawing the curves on top of them, or one of the other enlarging methods described in Chapter Three can be used (see pages 74-78).

2-22

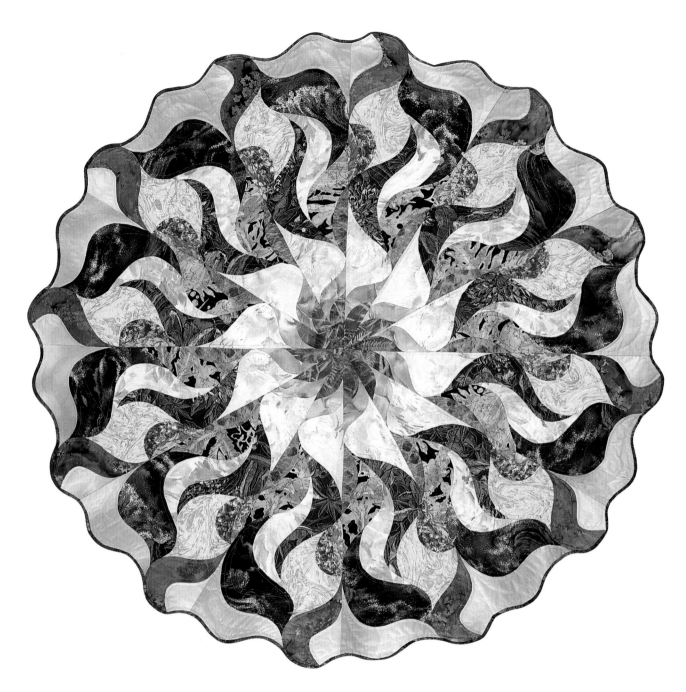

CAM AND KIRA'S WEDDING QUILT, 1994
60" diameter, *Judy B. Dales*

This quilt was a wedding gift for my oldest son and his bride and is a Curved
Kaleidomosaic design. Collection of *Cameron and Kira Dales*

# Curved Kaleidomosaics

## Geometric Structure

Once again we will be using a geometric structure as the basis for a curved design, but these designs are circular, so they produce totally different results. Back in the 1980s, I made a series of quilts using Islamic mosaic tile patterns. Islamic type patterns are found in many places around the world, can be drafted using only a straight edge and compass, and are suitable for adaptation to many art forms. The snapshots show tile floors in Venice, and the three books describe the geometry and philosophy involved in this type of drafting. The wooden box is a modern American interpretation of an Islamic design by craftsman Rob Nettleton of Eaton, New York.

Even though the patterns can be very complex, the drafting is quite simple. A circle is divided into equal portions, and a series of grids is laid over the basic structure. As additional lines are added, wonderful patterns emerge, and the challenge is to identify the specific ones that form repeating patterns and interesting shapes, the most predictable being stars. After I had begun working with curves, it occurred to me to try using the segmented circular structure as the basis for curved designs.

CAROUSEL WALTZ, 1987
72" diameter, *Judy B. Dales*

This quilt is the first I made using the Kaleidomosaic design approach. The curves used in a circular format produced a design with wonderful movement and grace. Collection of *William and Sandy Trice*. Photo: *Young Masters Studio*

The basic circle can be divided into any number of wedges, but I find ten or twelve to be the best. I used twelve wedges for the first several quilts, but have decided that narrowing it down to ten does not significantly alter the design and saves a lot of work. If you use fewer than ten wedges, the design begins to lose its flow and can take on a rather chunky effect. The entire ten-wedge circle is displayed here, so that you can see how it is drafted.

You will work with only one wedge, which is provided here in the small "designer" size of 6". Trace the 6" wedge out of the book and attach a tracing paper overlay. This exercise is similar to the two previous ones in that the geometric grid is there to help you get started, but you need not feel restricted by it in any way. In fact, you don't have to follow the grid very closely. Its function is merely to provide a few reference points.

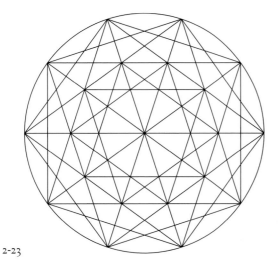

2-23

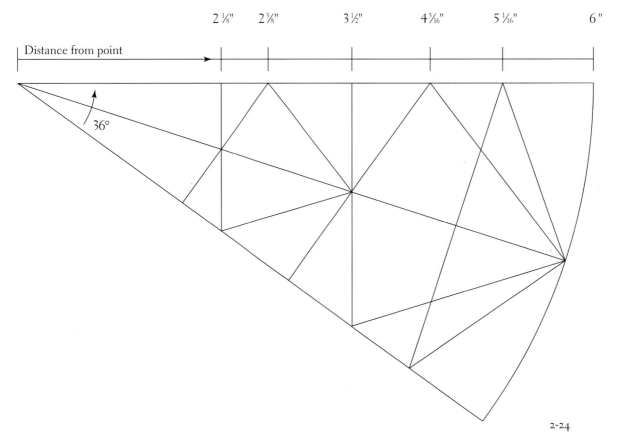

2-24

# Unique Properties of Curved Kaleidomosaics

There are several elements to be aware of as you work. Lines that flow out from the center produce a star burst effect (2-25 A and B), and lines that angle diagonally across the wedge will give the piece a circular, twirling motion (2-25 C and D).

2-25 A

2-25 C

2-25 B

2-25 D

You can work symmetrically within the wedge; that is, create a design that is a mirror image on either side of the center line, or you can choose to be more asymmetrical. The symmetrical designs are more static due to the way the design repeats, and a second mirror image will be produced at the boundaries of the wedge. I find the asymmetrical designs to be more pleasing because they tend to have more flow and movement. Keep in mind that when two wedges are placed side-by-side, secondary patterns will form. This is similar to what happens when two traditional blocks are joined, but the secondary design can be quite different in the circular format. It is not unusual for the secondary design to become the dominant design element, as is the case in the illustration below.

Lines added at the narrow point of the wedge doubles the number of seams intersecting in the center. Avoid this by making any lines coming down into the point merge with a side seam just before reaching the center, which creates an elegant flower or a star burst shape.

2-26 A

2-26 B

2-27 A
Twenty-four
seams in center

2-27 B
Twelve seams—
more manageable

2-27 C

In order to gain some experience with wedge repeats, sketch a very simple design and trace it several times to see how it behaves when repeated. Trace one wedge on a separate piece of paper several times, sliding the paper over to trace the multiples. Do not fold your original tracing paper to retrace your design, unless you specifically want a mirror image of the original design.

Illustration 2-28 B, shows the effect of sliding a wedge, and 2-28 C shows the same wedge, flipped one way, and then the other. In actuality, when you flip a wedge to reproduce it, you will automatically get an alternating combination of two patterns all around the design.

2-28 A

2-28 B

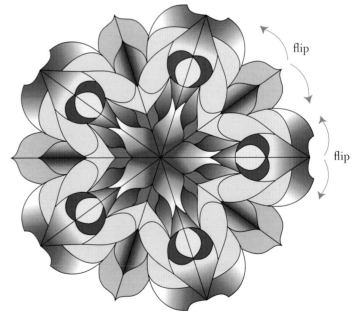

2-28 C

## Evaluate the Results

As with any block, you may want to adjust some of the lines on the edge of the wedge to avoid creating unsightly shapes when two pieces meet, or to help carry a line from one wedge to another. Remember that lines do not have to meet. Sometimes the design is more interesting if they don't, but a staggered line needs to look intentional. The lines that form the leaf shape in the narrow end of the wedge in 2-29A are close enough that they look as though they were intended to meet, but missed by just a little. Adjusting those lines so that they are further apart rectifies the situation and gives the center better definition, as seen in 2-29B. On the other hand, making the lines meet, as in 2-29C, creates a continuous flowing line that produces an entirely different effect. Neither option is right or wrong, it is merely a matter of preference.

The outer edge of a Kaleidomosaic design does not have to remain a plain circle. Scalloped or irregular edges (as seen on many of the illustrations here), can add a lot to the design. Keeping curves gentle and avoiding very sharp points and deep concave angles will allow you to bind the finished quilt without difficulty, but if you find that you have drawn something that looks problematic, read Chapter Six, page 119, on finishing. I have included instructions for finishing a quilt with a facing, which is one way to deal with difficult edges. The points and angles on the outer edge of this design create a great deal of its charm, so I would rather work a little harder to finish the edge than eliminate those elements. I think it is better that the design should challenge the sewer's technical expertise, rather than allowing technique to restrict the design.

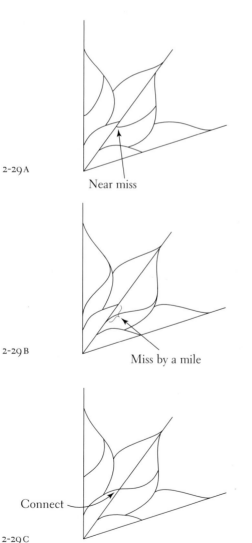

2-29 A

Near miss

2-29 B

Miss by a mile

Connect

2-29 C

2-30

I find that coloring the design can be helpful at this stage, because with Kaleidomosaic designs, it is not always clear which pieces will form the primary design, and which will become background. Sometimes the two are interchangeable. Coloring can help identify the various design elements, individual shapes, and repeating patterns, and can help separate foreground from background.

2-31A

2-31B

2-31C

The dominant part of the design can be altered dramatically when wedges are combined. In the single wedge (2-32A), the eye is drawn to the curved form in the center of the wedge. When wedges are combined (2-32B), the two large shapes on either edge combine to form a dramatic shape that competes for dominance. Sometimes the joining of two shapes is pleasing, as is the case here, but if the effect is not pleasant, lines need to be altered or added to break up the large shape.

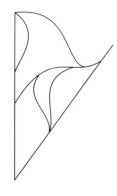

2-33A

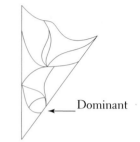

2-32A ·←—— Dominant

Focus changes when wedges are combined

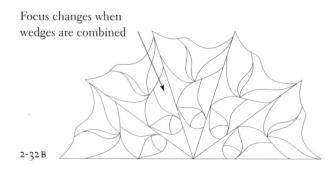

2-32B

2-33B

The overall balance of the design also needs to be evaluated. Is all the interest on the outer edge, leaving the center feeling weak? Or is the center so strong that you can hardly look at the rest of the design? It wasn't until I had the complete circle drawn that I realized the shape created in the center of this design was overpowering (2-33B). Even though most of the lines were in the outer areas, they were not strong enough to pull the attention away from the central section. The addition of one seam in each wedge creates a small star shape which decreases the size of the central figure so that it is more in proportion with the rest of the piece (2-33C).

2-33C

In order to fully evaluate your design, trace or copy your wedge enough times so that you have a complete circle. The single wedge (2-34A) looks unimpressive, but it actually has a lot of potential that is not revealed until you see the full circle. Two wedges combined are enough to discover that there are no awkward intersections or unwieldy secondary shapes, but you get very little feel for the design as a whole (2-34B). Half a circle reveals the rhythm of the design, but the eye yearns for more (2-34C). Finally, when all wedges are in place, the eye can travel all the way around, following the flow of lines and enjoying the rhythm of the design (2-34D). It is essential that the circle be complete, because an incomplete circle will always look unbalanced.

2-34A

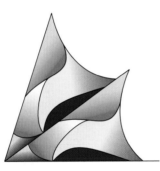

2-34B

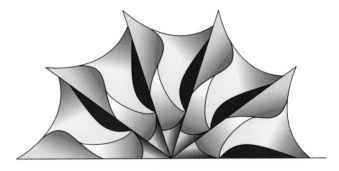

2-34C

2-34D

Fantasy Form #1634, 1995
57" x 40", *Judy B. Dales*

This piece is the first in a series of abstract curved designs that combine curved-seam piecing with layers of tulle and chiffon applied to the background to produce a watercolor effect.

# Free Form Designs
## Breaking Out of the Structure

Now that you've had a little experience working with curves, I hope that you are beginning to feel comfortable with them, and are excited at the wonderful effects they produce and the unlimited possibilities they offer. Perhaps you are even feeling a little restricted by the fact that the curves are being employed within a structured format. Well, now is the time to try some freehand curves, but before you begin, take a moment to prepare yourself.

## Teaching Your Brain About Curves

The primary purpose of these exercises is to practice drawing curves, and I encourage you to do this every day for a few weeks. The more you draw, the more comfortable you will feel with the whole process. Remember, at this point you aren't intending for your drawings to represent anything; you are just practicing.

You have already begun the process of famil-iarizing yourself with curves in the previous exercises, and each of the projects was a small step leading to this point. This exercise is similar to a form of physical therapy called patterning, and the intent is for your arm and hand to teach your brain everything it needs to know about curves.

*I have always envisioned my brain as a colander, heaped high with the infamous "gray matter." I sometimes feel that if I try to load too much new information into my colander, the pressure causes a certain amount of gray stuff to leak out the holes in the bottom of the colander! This would explain why so many things I used to know seem to be gone forever. When I lived in Germany in my thirties, I had to learn to speak the language very quickly. I imagined the whole process of learning a foreign language as being similar to forming a new path through the brain, a tunnel through all that gray stuff in my colander— sort of a "rotor-rooter" operation! And that is similar to what we need to do now: to create a special path in your brain for curves. You have already begun to form this path, but now we will really work on it.*

## Learning To Draw Is Easy When It's Curves

I have never thought of myself as a person who could draw. In fact, quilting appealed to me because it was an art form where drawing skills were not a prerequisite. However, in the ten years that I have been using curved images in my quilts, I have done a lot of drawing, and I have become quite good at it. You can too!

I can draw a graceful curve in one easy swoop, alter a curve ever so slightly to improve its appearance tremendously, and anticipate which curves will create graceful shapes. I can even demonstrate free form drawing in front of the class and produce what I think of as a "keeper," a design that is good enough to actually turn into a quilt!

My skill with curves is not something I was born with, nor is it the result of some genetic affinity. It is simply that in the past ten years I have drawn a lot of curves, and all that drawing has provided me with enough practice to get pretty good at it! You can do the same. Anyone can learn to draw (or paint, sew, weave, etc.) if they are willing to put in enough time and effort. Learning to draw curves is easier than any other kind of drawing for several very important reasons. First of all, remember that there is no such thing as a "right" or "wrong" curve. A curve can be sharp or tight, squiggly, graceful, ugly, sweeping, or delicate, but it can't be wrong. A curve is a curve is a curve! Don't be afraid of it!

The other comforting factor when working with curves is that the designs can be totally abstract. You don't have to produce something recognizable in order to create a beautiful design. So don't feel that you need to draw an actual object or a specific image—just draw curves in the beginning! Also keep in mind that your curves will improve with practice, so don't get upset if your first efforts aren't wonderful. You are learning a new skill, so you need to be patient with yourself.

## Preparation

For this exercise, I recommend a large pad of newsprint paper that is approximately 17" x 24". You can use other types (and sizes) of paper, but it needs to be inexpensive, so you won't be stingy with it. You will be doing a lot of practice drawing, and the more paper you use, the better your drawing will become. The individual sheets need to be large enough so that you can draw freely. The goal here is to loosen up, so you don't want to be cramped by lack of space. As you are working through the exercises, start with a fresh sheet of paper whenever you feel the need.

Choose a pencil that glides smoothly on the paper. A mechanical pencil can be too sharp and pointed and will sometimes dig into the paper, creating holes and totally disrupting the rhythm. A slightly dull standard pencil will probably work fine. Put your pencil to the paper and don't pick it up until you are finished with each exercise. In other words, don't stop to ponder, analyze, plot, or evaluate. Just keep that pencil moving!

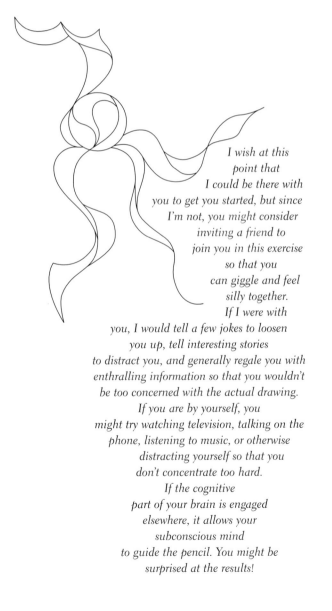

*I wish at this point that I could be there with you to get you started, but since I'm not, you might consider inviting a friend to join you in this exercise so that you can giggle and feel silly together. If I were with you, I would tell a few jokes to loosen you up, tell interesting stories to distract you, and generally regale you with enthralling information so that you wouldn't be too concerned with the actual drawing. If you are by yourself, you might try watching television, talking on the phone, listening to music, or otherwise distracting yourself so that you don't concentrate too hard. If the cognitive part of your brain is engaged elsewhere, it allows your subconscious mind to guide the pencil. You might be surprised at the results!*

## Circles and Curves

Begin by drawing circles. Draw both large and small circles, and try making them both clockwise and counterclockwise. Fill the whole paper with circles of various shapes, sizes, and descriptions. Draw slowly so that you can really feel the roundness. Use your whole arm, from the shoulder down. Stand up if it is more comfortable. Your drawing should be rhythmic and relaxed. You might even wish to hum a few bars of "The Skaters Waltz," or another favorite waltz tune. Remember that the purpose of this exercise is to create a curved path in your brain, to teach your brain about the feeling of "round" and "smooth." Be aware of how it feels to draw a nice, big round circle. It should feel good!

After you've drawn circles for a while, start with a fresh sheet of paper and draw curves. Begin with a big, fat S-curve right in the middle of the paper (a curve that goes up and then down, or left, then right, whichever orientation feels more comfortable). Trace over this curve, slowly and smoothly many times, imprinting the feel of it on your brain. After you feel very comfortable with this particular curve, branch out in another direction with a different curve. Don't lift your pencil, just meander over to a different spot. Retrace this second curve a number of times until it feels natural. Continue moving further and further afield, branching out in all directions. Try small, tight curves, large curves, squiggly ones, and smooth ones, remembering to draw slowly enough that your body and brain can experience the roundness. Fill the whole paper with curves and enjoy the graceful motion, as well as the beauty of what you are drawing.

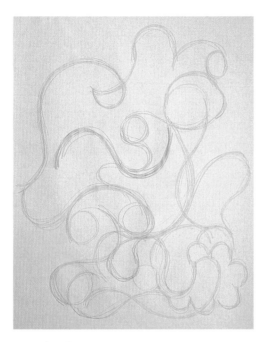

## Positive Thinking

If you notice negative notions creeping into your consciousness at this point, banish them at once. For example, if you think your efforts look like mere scribbles, you are being far too critical. Tell your little judge to go away! Remember that you are loosening up, learning something new, and you should be having fun. Don't spoil it with negative thoughts and over-critical reactions.

As your pencil is moving, you might keep in the back of your mind things that are curvy—waves, wings, clouds, teardrops, swirls, hair tendrils, flower petals— the list is endless. But don't try to draw something specific, just let the pencil meander. Keep your brain out of the activity! As your pencil moves over the paper, retrace lines and shapes until your hand can decide where to go next. It is important to keep the pencil moving and to keep the line continuous. If you stop and move the pencil to another point, or pause to plan where you will go next, you will lose the flow and give your brain an opportunity to invade the process.

## Shapes

When you start the next new paper, begin with curves, just as you did in the previous exercise, but this time think about forming shapes with your curves. In the last exercise, the lines were random and wandered all over the page, as they do in 2-35A. This time, try bringing the line back around so that the end of it connects with the beginning, forming a shape, as in 2-35B.

2-35A

2-35B

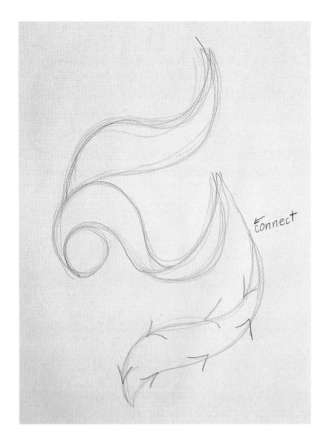

Try an S-curve first, retrace it several times, then draw another curve that bends back and connects with the beginning of the first one. Voila! You have produced a shape. The point here is that when you are designing for patchwork, you need shapes, or pieces, not just lines, so you need to think about creating the shapes as you go along. Don't think about just what those shapes will be at this point, just try to reconnect lines so that some kind of shape is formed.

## Unexpected Bonus

These exercises are merely the beginning of the process of drawing a design for quilt making, and the primary goal is to loosen up your arm and your brain. However, you should not overlook the possibility that you have created something usable. Examine your drawing and extract from the many scribbles the specific lines that form a pleasing design. Use a felt tip marker to darken the parts of the sketch that form graceful lines and interesting shapes.

Remember that all artists sketch first; they draw three or four different lines where they only want one, then they choose the line, or combination of lines, that looks best. This is a legitimate part of the drawing process. If you think of your drawing as being a sketch rather than random scribbles, it might help you to see its potential. You may be surprised at how attractive your design could be when translated into fabric!

Furthermore, there might be individual portions of a design that are quite appealing. Use tracing paper to extract these smaller motifs and repeat them in various positions to form an interesting pattern. The small segment (2-36A) was repeated to form the design in Illustration 2-36B.

2-36A

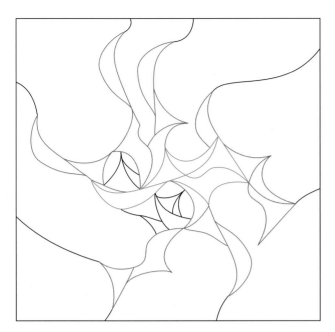

2-36B

After you have been doing this exercise for a while, you may see marked improvement in your scribbles. You may also begin to see recognizable images emerging, but if you do, consider them just a bonus. Remember that the primary goal is to learn to draw beautiful curves and interesting shapes. Don't try to force a design to become something specific. Stay loose and see what develops.

*I often find that drawings from a similar time frame all look the same—as if something were working very hard to get out of my subconscious. On one particular afternoon, every drawing looked like a spirit, or wood sprite. Other times, everything I draw seems to look grotesque. This is the reason, of course, that you have to keep drawing. If you do lots of sketches, the chance that one of them might be usable rises dramatically. And of course, your skill will improve with each one.*

HARMONY FLOWER, 1994
26" x 26", *Judy B. Dales*

This small quilt was the result of a challenge between the members of a design group
I belonged to. We each had very different taste in fabric, so when we all donated
two pieces of our favorite fabric to be used by the other members, it was indeed a
challenge to use all the diverse colors and types of prints in one piece.

# Cut Paper Designs
## Cut and Play

If the last exercise reminded you of a first-grade writing exercise, this one will transport you back to kindergarten, and it is just as much fun! Acquire several pieces of black construction paper. Cut one or two sheets of this paper into squares ranging from 3" to 5". (The exact measurements are not important.) Put three or four of the squares aside for later use.

From each of the squares cut a circle slightly smaller than the square. Save the paper that you have cut away because you may want a few straight lines in your design. You are now going to cut each circle into either three or four pieces. If you make three parallel cuts, you will divide the circle into three pieces. If you make one cut, then a second cut perpendicular to the first, you will be producing four pieces. The purpose here is to use either straight or curved cuts to produce the most varied and interesting shapes possible. Feel free to take more than the prescribed number of cuts, if necessary, to create interesting shapes.

You may find yourself cutting the same way each time, so concentrate on varying the cuts. Try to plan ahead a little bit so that you can make the most interesting and graceful shapes in a variety of sizes.

2-37 A

2-37 B

2-37 C

When you have a large pile of intriguing shapes, use them to form a design on a piece of 8 ½" x 11" white paper. Be adventurous and have fun with this exercise. Try lots of different combinations with various shapes, moving them around to explore different possibilities. I've discovered that once I get several pieces on the paper, I am reluctant to move them, or to add anything to them, for fear that I will lose what I've already created. Don't fall into this trap, but if you do, trace the placement of the shapes on the paper and then move on. The tracing ensures that you can return to the original design if you want to; however, it is better to just think positively, and convince yourself that change will surely produce an improvement. Photos 2-38A and B show how different a design can look after changing the placement of only one piece.

2-38 A

2-38 B

## Background Is Important Too

While you are moving your pieces around, be aware of the spaces and shapes that are formed by the white part of the design (the background). The shapes in 2-39A are graceful and interesting, but are not visually connected, giving the pieces a random appearance and making the design look disjointed. Moving them ever so slightly connects them visually, strengthens the design, and creates interesting shapes in the background (2-39B).

2-39 A

2-39 B

Also be aware of how your design is placed within the overall space created by the white paper. When the design is finished, you can make the overall space larger or smaller, but it is helpful to be aware of the total space as you work. As a general rule, a design should be slightly off-center (not exactly in the middle of the space), and it should be surrounded by the proper amount of background area to enhance, but not overwhelm, the main design elements.

2-40A

2-41A

2-40B

2-41B

The design in 2-40A could be quite a handsome rooster, but there is not enough background area to sustain the image. Conversely, the design in 2-40B looks insignificant because it is overwhelmed by too much background area.

Use strips of black paper to experiment with different frames for your design. Even a slight variation in size, shape, or the placement of the image within the frame can have a dramatic effect on the overall composition, as seen here in 2-41A and B.

## Repetition

Try to have some repetition of line and shape to give the design a sense of unity. If you find that you don't have two or three similar shapes, you can use the extra reserved squares to produce some. In fact, if you discover that none of your shapes are very attractive or inspiring, try cutting a few more. Now that you know what you will be doing with the shapes, it may be easier to cut interesting ones.

## Trust Your Instincts

As you play with your design, you may become aware of certain strong impulses. For example, you may have a strong urge to put a long skinny shape on the right side of your design, far away from the other pieces. Don't hesitate! Just do it! This is your innate, well-developed sense of balance at work! All of us have strong intuitive responses relating to principles of design, and we are instinctively aware of balance, emphasis, unity, or the lack thereof. In fact, the elements of design and the principles that govern them were devised to explain and clarify our very basic, normal human responses. The rules were not created to teach us how to respond, but rather, to explain the way we do respond, quite naturally. Unfortunately, many of us don't trust our instincts, but we should. Use this exercise to give your intuitive sense of composition a little exercise! If you feel strongly about something, follow that hunch. Nine times out of ten you will be right. And, of course, if you aren't, it's only a scrap of paper!

## Capture the Design

When you have a design that you like, lay a piece of tracing paper over it, being careful not to disturb anything, and trace around all the pieces. An alternate method is to carefully glue the pieces down before tracing, but I can never seem to do that without rearranging them slightly. The white paper can be sprayed lightly with spray glue before you begin, but be sure to use repositionable spray so that you can rearrange the shapes until you are pleased with the design. The disadvantage to using the spray is that the pieces are harder to move around, so I usually just use plain paper and trace the designs I like.

## Edit the Design

Next, you will need to turn the tracing into a usable pattern for piecing, which is a matter of refining the shapes and addressing technical difficulties. You will need to ease any curves that look too sharp and change any shapes that aren't quite right. Decide whether to keep a seam where one piece of paper overlaps another, or if it would be better to eliminate that seam and have one piece. Illustration 2-41A

shows a small detail extracted from the black and white silhouette design on the next page and shows the outline of the actual pieces. In 2-41B, the basic outline was retained, but different, more graceful lines were used, and the original ones discarded.

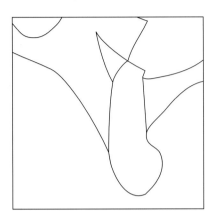

2-41A

2-41B

In Illustration 2-42B, the tracing shows only the rough outline of the shapes, but in 2-42C the seamlines have been added to break up the background area and to connect shapes, and larger shapes have been broken up and defined, while some of the curves have been adjusted. The final pattern (2-42D) shows where lines and shapes have been further refined to create a more graceful look.

It is wise to keep the original black and white cut-paper design at hand, which will help identify the original form that can be slightly obscured by the extra lines that have been added. Another approach is to render all added construction lines as broken lines, indicating that the shapes created by these lines are not a part of the original design.

2-42 A

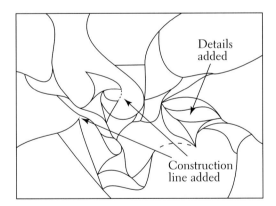

2-42 B

Details added

Construction line added

2-42 C   Background seams added

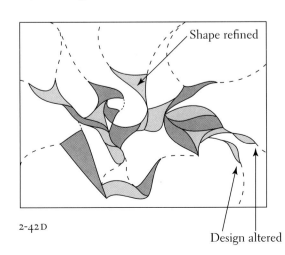

Shape refined

2-42 D

Design altered

In fact, when adding background and construction seams, which are there only to facilitate piecing, great care must be taken that the design is not altered significantly. In 2-43A, the seam that was added encloses an area of background space, which visually incorporates this space into the black figure. The lines that were added in 2-43B, however, leave this space free, more faithfully adhering to the original design. Even though many of these seams are added for technical reasons, none should look like an after-thought. They should be graceful lines, placed so that they enhance your composition and add to the overall beauty of the design.

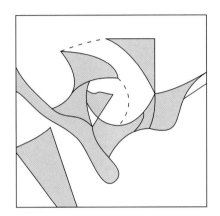

2-43 A

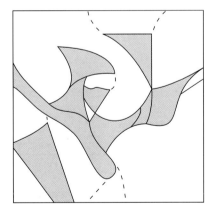

2-43 B

DAYLILIES, 1993
34" x 24", *Judy B. Dales*

This piece was made as a gift for two gardeners who love daylilies. Collection of *Judy and Bill Whitman*. Photo: *Ricardo Barras*

## Pictorial Designs
### Representational Designs

Another type of design that you may want to experiment with is pictorial, or landscape design. Using curves allows a much broader range of possibilities for patchwork, and the pattern and template method I've developed allow the use of almost any type of design. I keep a file of photographs and other inspirational images to use as design sources.

It is important, however, that you avoid using a copyrighted design. Some of the designs that are the most suitable for piecing are stylized drawings with simple clean lines, such as advertising logos, sketches in magazines, or the work of other artists. If you want to use such designs, you must either ensure that it is not copyrighted, or ask permission to use it if it is copyrighted. There is a great deal of confusion concerning copyright, but it is important to understand this issue so that you don't inadvertently do something unethical or illegal. It would be a shame to spend months working on a quilt, only to find out later that you can't exhibit or display it.

## Design Sources

So, where do you find source material for quilt designs? Your own photographs are a good place to start. Non-copyrighted art books are also a rich source. Try doing your own sketches and studies. Remember that it's not necessary to draw as well as Picasso to produce a drawing for patchwork, and learning to look at a subject and capture its essence is a skill that can be learned with practice. There are many books that explain how to develop a design, as well as those that offer copyright-free designs on a wide variety of topics. If you begin to search, you will find that inspiration and design assistance are everywhere.

## Enlarging the Design

Once you have found a suitable design source, the next step is to alter and enlarge it to the proper size. Let's use a photograph that I took myself as an example. Trace only the main lines of the design, just enough to ensure that you have the proper proportions. Adding details to a picture is usually not difficult once the main proportions are established.

After you have decided on the size of the finished project, enlarge the design, using any one of the methods discussed in Chapter Three (see pages 74-78), make any refinements that are necessary, and add the details. Don't forget that the easiest way to sew a landscape may be to piece the major parts of the design and add the details with appliqué. For many years I felt compelled to accomplish everything with piecing, but I have mellowed a bit, and now think that the best way is the easiest way, whatever that happens to be.

2-44

# Chapter Three

# From Design to Pattern

## Evaluate the Design
### Check It Out
Each of the different design approaches have required some evaluation during the process, but a final, general evaluation needs to be done at this point before a pattern is created. Your design may be a rough sketch (as in 3-1) from which you have extracted a design (as in 3-2), which will need some polishing and refining, both from an aesthetic and technical standpoint.

3-1

3-2

The design in 3-2 has a number of elements that need to be refined and corrected before it can be a sewable pattern, including some very sharp curves, a few dangling points, a lot of seams intersecting at one place, and large background areas that need to be broken up.

## Edit the Curves
Carefully check the curves, lines, and shapes in your design. Are the curves smooth and graceful, and not too sharp? After years of experience, I can draw a pretty nice curve, but I still spend a lot of time refining each line in a design, ensuring that each is as lovely as possible. A fraction of an inch can make a big difference where curves are concerned. Notice that I have very subtly altered some of the lines when tracing them from the original doodle.

When evaluating curves, it is necessary to take note of not only how they look, but also how they will be to sew. Are some of the curves so sharp as to be unmanageable? If so, they can probably be smoothed out a bit without altering the design significantly. In reality, almost any curve can be pieced, including a complete circle, but sharper ones do require more effort. Each quilter needs to evaluate her sewing skills, and decide for herself where she wants to make alterations that will ease the piecing process. A little practice sewing of curves at this point may indicate your skill level, which can be helpful when designing your own pattern.

STUDIO VIEW, 1992
40" x 20", *Judy B. Dales*

This design is from a photograph I took from my studio window in our house in
northern New Jersey and is a scene that I dearly miss, now that we live elsewhere.
After a long day at the sewing machine or the drawing board, the spectacular
sunsets were a pleasant way to end the workday. I often bring this quilt with me
when I travel to teach, because I would like to dispel some of the negative
impressions my fellow Americans have about the state of New Jersey. It is actually
a very beautiful state. Photo: *Ricardo Barras*

## Troubleshooting

If there is any spot in your design (other than the
focal point) that continually draws attention to itself,
take a careful look at it to determine why this is so.
It is very annoying to have one's attention constantly
diverted by one nagging element. The problem might
be an awkward curve, a grotesque shape, an overly
large piece, or a disparate shape, but whatever it is,
it needs to be fixed now. A design flaw cannot easily
be rectified with clever fabric use. In fact, such a
flaw will make it more difficult, if not impossible, to
choose fabric for that area of the design.

*Many quilters are quite
intimidated by curves and
think they do not have
the necessary
sewing experience
to deal with
them. This,
however, is often not
the case. Sewing a curved
seam in patchwork
is very much like setting
in a sleeve on a blouse or
shirt, which many quilters
have done. When put
in this perspective,
the idea of sewing curves
becomes less threatening.*

Be aware, however, that every time you change a line, or add a line, there will be repercussions on both sides of the line. When you alter a line, you may be greatly improving the shape on one side, and ruining the shape on the other. The same is true if you add a line to break up a large shape, such as the one in the upper central portion of the design shown in Illustration 3-2 (page 62). The gray straight line added in 3-3A is definitely not right. A curved line is a better choice, but the red curved line produces a nice shape on the left side of the line, but not on the right. Bringing the end of the line to point B instead of point A, as in 3-3B, makes this line more interesting, but not quite right. When the red line makes one long gradual curve it produces a nice effect. However, the bulge at the bottom of this new shape is not very attractive. Redrawing the bottom line corrects the problem, as well as easing the sharp point at A, which will make the sewing easier.

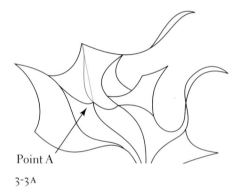

Point A

3-3A

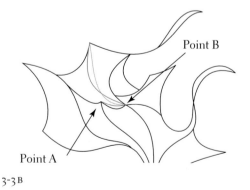

Point B

Point A

3-3B

In addition, the two long skinny points in the upper right were eliminated in 3-4 because they were not actually adding much to the design. In the process, the line on the right was changed to smooth out the sharp curve.

3-4

## Background Checks

The alteration created in Illustration 3-4 acts as a reminder that other seams need to be added to the background area. These are important, not only to make the sewing of points in your design easier, but to break up the large expanse of space. While their main function is technical, it is important that these lines be aesthetically pleasing, so care needs to be taken to ensure that they work well in the design and enhance the overall effect you are trying to achieve.

3-5

After the background seams are added, check again to see that there are no unconnected lines or shapes, which for some unaccountable reason I call "pigs in space." You definitely don't want any of these in your design, because an unconnected line fails to create a shape, so it can't be pieced, and an unconnected shape often creates an unpieceable point, like the one in 3-6A. Draw a line to connect the "pig in space" to some other point in the design. It is important that you don't inadvertently create a new shape when you add this line, as was done in 3-6B. Care must be taken to connect it in the right place, as was done in 3-6C.

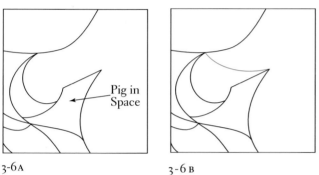

3-6A

3-6B

3-6C

It is important that the amount of background in your design is appropriate for the size of the main design. Put a large piece of tracing paper over the design and experiment with different sizes and shapes, or use four strips of paper to create a suitable frame for the design. In 3-7A, the design is situated so there is an appropriate amount of background space. In 3-7B, the borders are pulled in much too close, so there is less background space, and the design looks crowded. In 3-7C, the space is even tighter, and now the design works better in a horizontal format, but some of the lines will need to be altered to accommodate this new format.

3-7A

3-7B

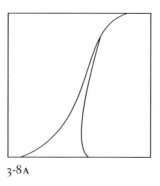

3-7C

## Points and Intersections

Are the intersections where one line meets another smooth, with one line gradually melding into another, or are they abrupt and awkward looking? Occasionally lines need to be altered, not only to make them more graceful, but also more sewable. For example, a line merging gradually into another line makes a sharp point (3-8A), which is actually easier to sew than a line that curves sharply inward and intersects bluntly (3-8B). The sharp point just happens naturally when the two seams are sewn accurately as marked, so two smoothly intersecting lines are a much better choice.

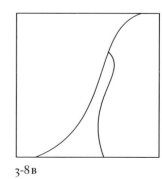

3-8A

3-8B

In the same vein, two lines coming to a point with a line extended, as in 3-9A, are easier to sew than the rounded tip in 3-9B. Quilters will often draw the sharp curve in lieu of a point, because they have been conditioned to think points are difficult. Not only is the point easier to sew than a curve, but it is nicer looking as well, and the extended line can be rendered barely noticeable by using the same fabric on either side of it.

If there are too many seams intersecting in one place, a slight alteration of a few of the lines can eliminate the problem. Simply move the intersection of some of the seams away from the major intersection. Merging the curved lines a slight distance away from the major intersection will not alter the appearance of the design, but will stagger the seams, thus making the sewing much easier.

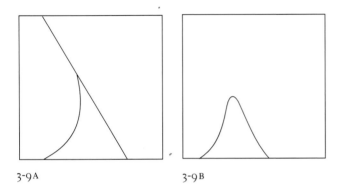

3-9A                    3-9B

3-10A                    3-10B

People are always amazed by the skinny pieces and sharp points in this quilt (full view shown on page 63), not knowing how simple they really are! This entire quilt is pieced, but I have often had people argue that fact with me. The tree trunks look as though they were appliquéd because they seem to be lying on top of the background. They have that appearance because I very carefully and intentionally pressed them so that they would look that way.

DETAIL OF STUDIO VIEW
Photo: *Ricardo Barras*

*You may be surprised at the recognizable images that can appear when you are working with curves. However, sometimes they can be embarrassingly suggestive, so it's best to correct those shapes before you start working with fabric! You might wish to share your design with a friend, who may see things that you have overlooked. I am always amazed at the things people see in my designs— often there are shapes and images of which I was totally unaware. I'm grateful that, so far, none of them have been too suggestive or embarrassing.*

THE FLEET, 1997
35" x 43", *Judy B. Dales*

After the sailboat motif was drawn, I photocopied it so that
I could experiment with different sizes and formations.
I like this arrangement because it seems to be an aerial
view of the fleet heading out to open water.

WEST WITH THE NIGHT, 1987
78" x 36", *Judy B. Dales*

The inspiration for this quilt was a simple bird design, which I placed in different shaped blocks. Initially I had
difficulty with the design, until I realized that each of the birds was encapsulated in its own isolated space, and
they were all traveling westward. It was then that I realized the connection with Beryl Markham's compelling
description of her historic solo flight across the Atlantic Ocean, traveling from east to west. The description of her
feeling of isolation in the small cockpit, with only the instrument lights to relieve the total darkness, was an image
that stayed with me. When I made the connection between her book, *West With the Night* and the work in
progress, the design almost floated together. Notice how carefully the blocks were placed to create a balanced
composition. Collection of *Cameron and Kira Dales*. Photo: *Young Masters Studio*

## Composition
### Balance

Check to make sure that your design is balanced. Some designs are perfectly balanced, because they are exactly the same from side to side and from top to bottom, as in 3-11. This design is said to have formal balance because it is quadrilaterally symmetrical; that is, exactly the same in each quarter of the design. However, notice that the actual block unit from which the design is created is not symmetrical.

The design in 3-12 is not symmetrical, but the blocks have been placed very carefully to create a balanced design.

Other designs are not formally balanced, so special effort is required to ensure that the different elements create an overall feeling of balance, even though there is no actual symmetry. The design of *The Fleet*, shown on the previous page, is well balanced because most of the visual weight is at the bottom and concentrated just a little bit off-center.

If you feel the tendency to tilt your head as you view your design, it may be visually heavier on one side than the other. An example of this would be 3-13A, where the majority of the shapes are concentrated on the left side, leaving mostly background on the right side. This pulls the visual weight too far to the left, which creates an unbalanced feeling that can be quite unsettling. A disturbing feeling can also be produced if the main point of interest is too far from the center, or if the top of your design is visually heavier than the bottom.

While it is not considered a good idea to put an object, or group of objects, directly in the center of your design (because this is where you would expect to find it and the predictability detracts from the overall effect), care must also be taken not to place it too far from the center. When the focal point is placed slightly off-center, this creates a bit of tension that makes the design more interesting. However, if the focal point is moved too far from the center, as in 3-13A, it becomes a distraction and causes the composition to look unbalanced. In 3-13B, one boat has been placed in the far right corner. This does a great deal to balance the scene. The one boat carries a lot of visual weight, not only because it is all alone, but also because it is a great distance from

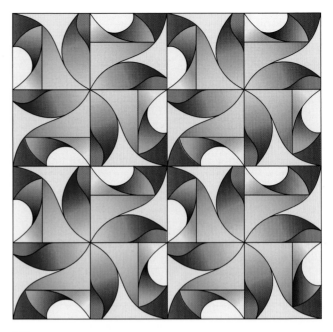

3-11

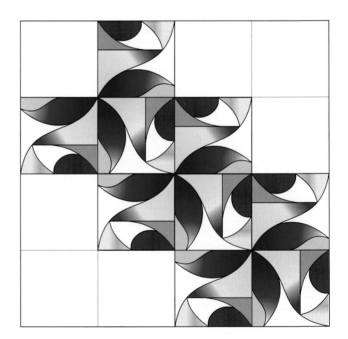

3-12

the center of the picture. The farther an object is from the center of the composition, the more it will draw your eye, which is what gives it "visual weight" and enables it to balance the five other boats.

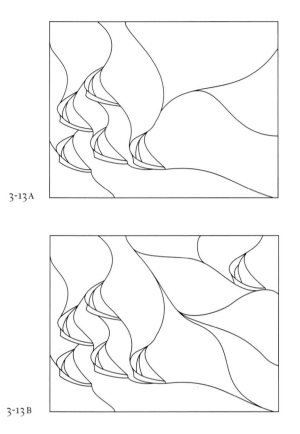

3-13A

3-13B

Most of us have a well developed sense of balance, and may experience discomfort when confronted with an unbalanced design. We may not, however, realize what the problem is until we actually start to analyze the source of the discomfort. Learn to trust your instincts. If you feel something is disturbing, it probably will be for others as well, and should be changed.

We humans like to see the heaviest elements on the bottom of a composition, because that is what our eye is accustomed to seeing in nature. When we look at the horizon, the ground is on the bottom with the light, airy sky on the top. If we look at a structure, the largest part is usually on the bottom, supporting the rest of it. If it is not—if the top is appearing bigger and heavier—we perceive this to be precarious, a catastrophe waiting to happen, and this makes us nervous. We transfer this intuitive response into our reactions to art, and feel uncomfortable if most of the visual weight is at the top of a composition.

In an attempt to give the impression that the boats are sailing into the distance, they were all placed at the top of the picture in 3-14A. Even though there was a very good reason for the placement, it still creates a feeling of unease. In 3-14B, more waves added to the bottom of the picture help to visually support the boats. As a line drawing, the number of lines seems overwhelming; but in actuality, fabrics of similar colors and values could be used, with perhaps a slight shading toward darker values at the bottom, so that the number of individual waves would not seem so overwhelming (but would still support the top of the picture). Another solution, as in 3-14C, would be to move the fleet of boats away from the top portion of the picture, which would help the balance.

3-14A

3-14B

3-14C

## Repetition and Variety

If a person looking at a quilt discovers one piece of fabric that she particularly likes, she will automatically search for more of it elsewhere in the quilt. This is because human beings like repetition; it is soothing and reassuring to find similar colors, shapes, angles, or motifs in artwork. However, taken too far, repetition produces boredom. If too much of the same fabric (or the same shape or color) is used, its appearance becomes routine, and the elements of discovery and surprise are completely lost. The monotony discourages the viewer, who loses interest and moves on to more exciting images. Therefore it is important to find a satisfying balance between repetition and variety.

Even though repetition is usually a good thing, almost anything will be boring if it is repeated over and over, as in 3-15 A. The viewer need not look at each object individually because it quickly becomes apparent that they are all identical.

Adding even the slightest bit of variety, such as varying the placement of the objects, as was done in 3-15 B, improves the composition immediately and creates more interest. Making changes to the objects themselves, as was done in 3-15 C, introduces more variety. Changing the size, color, or details of an object means that the viewer must look at all of them because of the variety.

As more variety is introduced, the composition becomes more interesting. In 3-15 D, the objects are not only different sizes, but reverse images have been introduced, and the placement of the objects is also varied. However, in 3-15 E, suddenly there seems to be too much variety, and now the boats seem to be wandering aimlessly, and the impression is one of chaos. Even though the actual boat image has not changed, the size, direction, and placement of the objects has been varied, and the repetition of the image is not enough to balance all the other changes. There must be balance between repetition and variation in order to have a good composition.

3-15 A    No variation

3-15 B    Placement variation

3-15 C    Size variation

3-15 D    Size, placement, and
direction variations

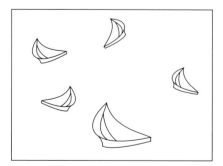

3-15 E    Chaotic

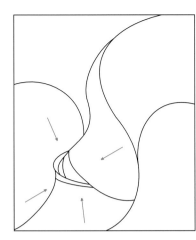

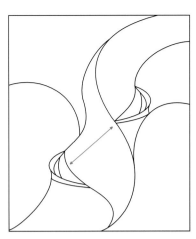

3-16A    One domineering element    3-16B    Two competing elements    3-16C    Three harmonious elements

Another argument for having a little repetition in your design is the fact that anything, if it is all alone, will attract undue attention to itself and look out of place. If a whole scrap quilt is created with soft grayed colors, one little touch of hot pink would draw the eye and become a distracting element. The same is true for any different or unusual element, such as the one, lone sailboat in 3-16A. It is very annoying to have your eye continually dragged back to this one domineering element. The obvious solution to this dilemma would be to remove the offending element, but a more creative suggestion is to add more! By incorporating more of the element, it will no longer be alone, or so dominant, but the addition of a second boat in 3-16B does little to remedy the situation. Now the eye is bounced back and forth between the two boats like a tennis ball, and this is hardly a pleasant experience.

The solution is to have a number of the eye-catching elements scattered about, which will serve to move the eye around the composition. When a third boat is added in 3-16C, the eye can begin a circular motion as it moves from boat to boat. Three of anything is usually sufficient to stimulate this circular movement, but a larger odd number might be even better.

## Focal Point

Every design needs a focal point, which is a place that the eye returns to again and again as it moves around the design. In a medallion quilt, the focal point is quite obviously the central motif, or the medallion.

In a painting, the focal point can be the central figure, or the big red barn that dominates the scene, or the one lone flower, and generally, the other elements in the painting are arranged to gently lead your eye back to that focal point.

Interestingly, many quilt designs do not have an actual focal point, being more of a repeat pattern than a composition, so we quilters are not accustomed to thinking about focal points. Therefore, it may be necessary to really study your design, taking note of how, and where, the eye travels. The eye should eventually cover all areas, but there should be one place that dominates slightly. The three sailboats in 3-17A form a strong focal point, not only because they are grouped together, but also because the background lines have been carefully placed to lead your eye around the composition continually bringing it back to the boats. The composition in 3-17B, however, has no focal point. The eye wanders everywhere, and the design appears chaotic and unfocused.

3-17A    Strong focal point    3-17B    No focal point

## Unity

I'm sure that we have all, at one time or another, seen a quilt whose border looks so different from the main part of the quilt that it looks as though the border had been temporarily borrowed from another piece. This is an example of lack of unity. The effect could perhaps be remedied by carrying certain colors, shapes, or motifs from the center to the borders, thus ensuring that there was some logical connection between the two.

Repetition is one of the elements that gives a design unity. A collection of disparate elements must have something to connect them in order to form a good composition, and repetition of one element, such as color, shape, or line, is often what pulls a design together. It is important to remember that none of the rules of composition stand alone. They are all interrelated and must work together to create a good composition.

All parts of a design need to be integrated so that even if the individual elements are very different from each other, they still seem to belong together. If you wish to incorporate a straight-edged shape into a curved design, there needs to be some method of integrating it into the whole design. The triangles in the design in 3-18A look out of place because there is no justification for them to be there. In 3-18B, the triangles are better integrated simply because of their placement in the design. Making the triangles less rigid by curving their sides, as in 3-18C, helps to integrate them into the design even more. However it is accomplished, the triangles must be made to look as though they belong there, rather than appearing to have ended up there by chance or as an afterthought.

3-18A

3-18B

3-18C

Snowscene, 1990
67" x 43", *Judy B. Dales*

This impressionistic scene began life as an appliquéd landscape that I had envisioned
in a horizontal format. But no matter how many times I rearranged the layers, the
scene came out square. I was so frustrated by this lack of control that I allowed
the finished top to languish in my studio for months. I finally decided to cut it up
and fragment it by inserting random strip piecing. Not only did this provide me with
a whole new technique, but it solved the size and shape problem. Since then I have
done more of these fragmented landscapes, such as the one on page 127, but now
I piece the simple landscape before it is segmented. Collection of *Sarah Youngblood.*
Photo: *Young Masters Studio*

# Enlarging the Design

## Design Clean-up

Once you are satisfied with your design, go over the lines with a fine, felt-tip marker to darken the lines and clean up the design. This process forces a number of issues. It makes you choose once and for all which line is best, or decide exactly where you want an intersection point to fall. However, keep in mind that even if you make a dreadful mistake at this point, there is always the option of more tracing paper and a fresh start. Nothing is ever final! In fact, if your first drawing is messy (lots of erasures, smudge marks, and changes), it might just be easier to retrace it than to clean it up. As always, choose the quickest and easiest route.

## Determining the Appropriate Size

The process of determining the correct size is a difficult one that involves a lot of different criteria and a bit of trial and error. The size, shape, and number of pieces in the design are important. Obviously, a design with a great many pieces works better as a larger design, and one with a relatively few number should probably be quite small, but the size of the individual pieces should also be taken into consideration. If you compare the quilt *Seasons of the Heart* (page 109) with *Buds* (page 115), it should be obvious why one is a very large quilt and the other is quite small.

If you enlarge a design too much, the pieces will look grotesque, and the design becomes so diffused that it becomes aimless and incoherent. If a design is too small, it can look cluttered and overly fussy. Keep in mind that the smaller a design is, the harder it will be to sew. Not only are the individual pieces smaller, but the curves will be tighter, and thus more difficult to piece than the gradual ones.

Consideration also needs to be taken to the proportionate size of the pieces. There should be some size variety, of course, but too much disparity can make deciding on the appropriate size difficult. If the smallest pieces dictate a rather large design, some of the larger pieces may end up too large. Large pieces can be filled with large scale fabric, of course, but I have discovered that it is difficult to correct a design problem with fabric. It's better to address and correct design issues before you start working with fabric, and often the easiest solution to this problem is to add a few lines to break up the overly large pieces and bring them into proper proportion with the rest of the quilt. Such was the case with the design in Illustration 2-42 C on page 59 in the previous chapter. The large "bud" shape on the right side was a good deal larger than the others in the design. Adding three lines not only broke the shape into smaller pieces, but enhanced the impression of a bud.

There is definitely a bit of guesswork involved in determining the proper size, but don't be discouraged by this. Time spent now getting your design perfected is time well spent. The process of making a quilt is very time consuming, and you certainly don't want to spend all that time putting together a design that isn't right to begin with. So be patient and keep at it until you get it right. Enlarging any quilt design can be one of the most daunting steps in the design process, but fortunately there are easy ways to accomplish this thanks to modern technology.

## Different Approaches

The previous exercises have produced many different types of finished designs, some of which require slightly different enlargement methods. For instance, the easiest way to enlarge a drawing inspired by one of the blocks shown on page 21, or a group of blocks, such as the ones shown on pages 32-35 is to enlarge the supporting straight-line block to the appropriate size and then reproduce the curved lines exactly as you drew them on the small drawing. Keep in mind that if the curved design is quite intricate, the finished design should probably be larger than the usual 12" block size.

When you analyze your free-form drawings and cut-paper designs, you may discover that you were lucky enough to create them in a size that can be directly translated into fabric. If not, they will have to be enlarged using one of the following methods. Kaleidomosaic designs are created in a small format and require a specialized approach.

## Enlarging a Wedge

Kaleidomosaic designs require that the individual wedge be scaled up to the appropriate size without altering the basic proportions. Because the individual wedges will be pieced together to form a complete circle, it is imperative that the angle at the wedge's inner point be accurate. The angle will not be altered when the size is increased; only the radius (length of the edges) increases. The number of degrees for the angle when a circle is divided into ten segments is 36°, and for twelve segments, the angle would be 30°. A protractor could be used to draw the appropriate angle, or simply trace the wedge out of the book and extend the edge lines as far as necessary. Use a sharp pencil and work carefully to ensure that the angle is reproduced exactly.

The next step is to reproduce the straight-line grid, used in the original "designer" wedge, which will enable you to draw a larger design with the same proportions as your small one. The original measurements on the 6" edge of the "designer" wedge that were used for creating the grid are shown in Illustration 2-24 on page 40. Illustration 3-19A on this page gives the edge measurements for drawing a grid in a wedge with a radius of 18", which would yield a 36" wallhanging. Illustration 3-19B shows the measurements for a wedge with a radius of 24", which would yield a 48" wallhanging. After you have traced the wedge angle from the book and extended the edge lines, use the given measurements to make marks at the indicated distance from the point. Use these marks to reproduce the grid, and then the curved design can be redrawn over it in the larger size.

If you wish to make a wallhanging of different dimensions than the ones given, simply multiply the measurements on the 6" wedge (page 40) by the appropriate number. For example, if you want a 60" wallhanging, divide by 2 to find out how large the wedge radius should be (in this case it would be 30"). Divide 30 (size of wedge you need) by 6 (size of designer wedge) to find the enlargement factor, which would be 5. Multiply all the measurements on the designer wedge by 5 to figure the distances to measure up the edges on the larger wedge, which will enable you to draw the proper grid.

Distance from point   6⅜"   7⅞"   10½"   12¹⁵⁄₁₆"   15³⁄₁₆"   18"

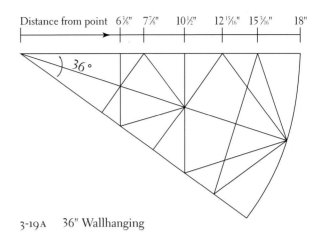

3-19A    36" Wallhanging

Distance from point   8½"   10⅞"   14"   17¼"   20¼"   24"

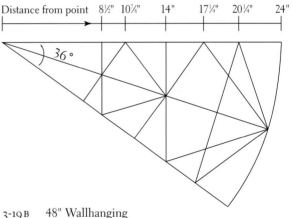

3-19B    48" Wallhanging

## Professional Copying

One of the easiest methods of enlargement is to take the design to a well-equipped copy store and have it enlarged. Many of the larger chains of copy stores have machines that can handle a design of any length and a width of 36". You may be able to break your design into segments that will fit on this machine, but a little math will be required to figure out the size each segment needs to be.

If your local copy shop does not have a machine that can handle large sizes, your design can be broken down into sections and copied piece by piece on a regular-sized machine, then reassembled with tape. This can be tedious and confusing, but a good copy technician ought to be able to help you. Be aware that an enlargement is not always an exact replica of the original, because the machines often enlarge more in one direction than the other. You may have to make slight adjustments to some lines when the enlarged copies are reassembled, but this method will at least provide the major proportions of the design.

I have had large scale designs copied at a blue-print shop, and if you do some research, you may find a specialty graphics shop in your area that can enlarge designs. However, once again, you may discover that 36" is the largest width. The disadvantages to using any kind of copying method is that it can be quite costly, and it requires some advance planning. Since I generally want to enlarge something at midnight, I have found other methods work better for me.

## Overhead Projector

By far, the easiest way to enlarge a design is to use an overhead projector (not to be confused with a slide projector). An overhead projector allows anything printed on a 8½" x 11" sheet of transparent plastic to be projected onto a screen or the wall. Look for a second-hand machine, or perhaps your quilt guild would be interested in owning one and making it available to all the members. Schools, libraries, hotels, and convention centers often have this type of equipment available, and you may be able to borrow or rent one from them.

In order to use this method of enlargement, the design needs to be the same size as a standard piece of paper, so sometimes it is necessary to reduce the size of the drawing before the actual enlargement process begins. Either use a copy machine to transfer the design onto transparency film, or trace the design onto write-on film with a marker that marks on plastic. Transparency film for use with a plain paper copier is different than the write-on film used only for overhead projectors, so be sure you have the correct kind before running it through the copier.

Once the design is transferred to the transparency, you can place this on the overhead projector and project it on the wall in any size. I try to "guesstimate" how large the design should be, and draw the appropriate sized rectangle or square on a piece of graph paper that is taped to the wall. Then I can move the projector back and forth until the projected image fits into the drawn square or rectangle. It is important that the projector be absolutely perpendicular to the wall and level with the paper. If it is not aligned properly the image will not be square.

Use a pencil to lightly trace the lines. Don't worry too much about reproducing each line perfectly at this point. The goal is to get the major shapes and the proper proportions on the paper.

The first time I used this method, I had a bit of trouble finding the proper size. My first effort looked fine when I projected it, but when I took the traced pattern to my studio, I realized it was too large. My second try turned out to be too small. The third time it turned out just right! Luckily, it doesn't take long to trace the design, so I didn't waste too much time or effort, but I was rather perplexed that I had miscalculated so badly. I have learned not to trust my impression of the projected image on the wall. I try, instead, to determine how big the piece should be before I project it.

## Grid Enlargement

The good, old-fashioned grid system of enlargement is one that I think of as a last resort. It's a method I think everyone should know how to do, but it is a tedious process at best. However, it need not be quite as tedious as you may have thought. I have discovered that I can usually draw the enlarged design quite easily if I remember to *redraw* it, rather than copy or reproduce it. If I drew the small design, it would seem logical that I could draw it again larger, and keeping that fact in mind seems to make the whole process a little easier. There may be a few changes that occur in the process, but I have discovered that the changes in the larger drawing are usually an improvement, due, I suppose, to the fact that it is easier to draw curves on a larger scale. Worry less about reproducing the small drawing exactly, and focus instead on making the large drawing graceful and flowing.

Begin the enlargement process by measuring the small design and superimposing a 1" grid over it, either with a colored pencil or a regular pencil, and a tracing paper overlay. The design in 3-20A is 7" wide and 9" tall and is gridded in 1" increments. Decide how much larger you want the finished quilt to be. In the example, the enlargement is twice as big, so the square is drawn out 14" wide and 18" tall, and covered with a grid where each square is 2". Each 1" square on the smaller drawing corresponds to a 2" square on the larger one, and numbering the squares the same makes it easier to refer from one to the other.

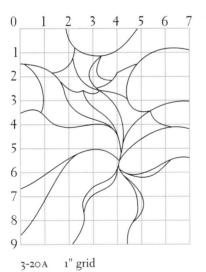

3-20A    1" grid

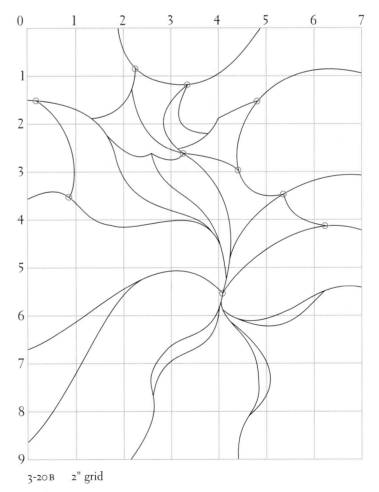

3-20B    2" grid

If you want the enlargement to be five times bigger, multiply the measurements by five, draw the rectangle 35" by 45", and mark with a 5" grid. Each 1" square on the small drawing corresponds to a 5" square on the enlargement.

As you begin to transfer your drawing, don't try to reproduce each line inch for inch. Start by finding important intersection points, such as the tips of the leaf-type shapes and the place where all the lines intersect in the example. Find and mark all of these important points by counting squares over and down (or up, as the case may be), and then simply draw in the connecting lines freely and quickly.

Remember, you are redrawing the design larger, not actually copying it line for line. Sketch the lines lightly with pencil and refer to the small design if you need to check how far out a line curves, or how far a point extends, but think of it as reassurance only. Your large drawing may not duplicate the small one exactly, and that is perfectly all right. When the entire design is sketched and you are happy with it, redraw the lines darker with a felt-tip marker and erase any excess sketched pencil lines.

Once the design is enlarged, it needs to be evaluated one more time. It is quite possible that you will see things in the larger drawing that were obscure in the smaller version. Perhaps some of the pieces are out of proportion, or perhaps a line could be improved. Make sure that lines intersect crisply, and that you have eliminated any sketch lines and have just one clean line.

# Creating the Master Pattern
## Template Labeling

When you have a good, clean drawing, it is time to mark the pattern with suitable symbols. The first step is to label all the pieces in some sort of logical manner. I give each piece a number designation, or a letter, or a combination of both. These labels indicate in which part of the pattern the piece belongs. For instance, the letter B usually indicates background, an F might indicate flower or form. I usually start numbering in the upper left corner and work around in a clockwise direction, so that when I pick up a template, there will be a hint as to where that particular piece belongs.

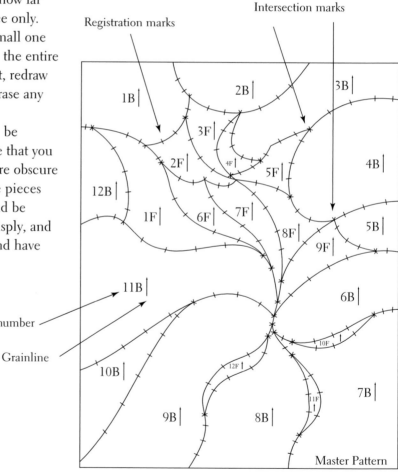

3-21

## Intersection Marks

An important mark that needs to be added to the master pattern is what I call an intersection mark, which shows where seams begin and end. If two seams cross at right angles, there is no question where the seams end or begin because there are obvious corners to indicate this, as in 3-23. However, when a seam intersects on only one side of a line, as in 3-24, it is helpful to have a mark on the opposite side of the line that indicates exactly where that intersection should be. A little "v" on the flat side of the line will indicate that a seam intersects there (3-24B).

Furthermore, when a seam merges gradually with another seam, there is often no perceptible angle or corner on either seam to indicate exactly where it should end, as is the case in 3-25. Marking a "v" on either side of the intersection will give this information. The two "v"s together often appear to be an "X", but when the templates are cut apart, they will revert to a "v." These marks are transferred to the seam allowance on the back of the fabric, thus making it very clear where seams begin and end.

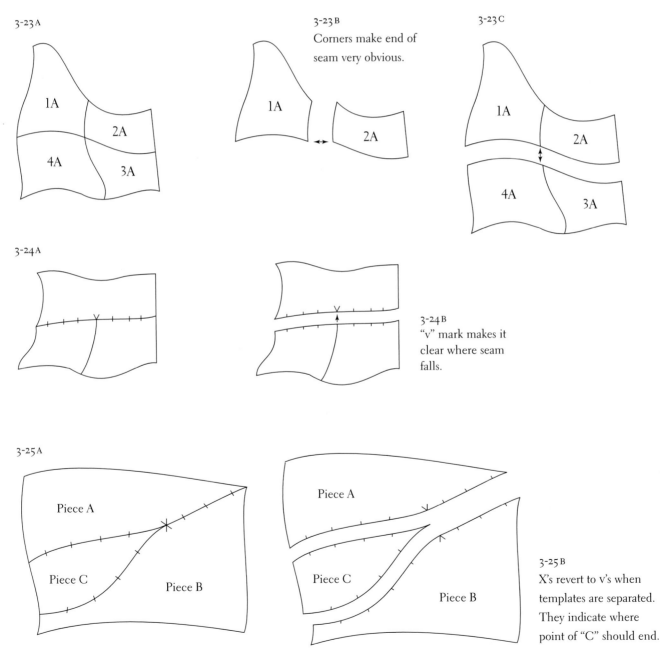

3-23 A

3-23 B
Corners make end of seam very obvious.

3-23 C

3-24 A

3-24 B
"v" mark makes it clear where seam falls.

3-25 A

3-25 B
X's revert to v's when templates are separated. They indicate where point of "C" should end.

## Grainlines

Each pattern piece also needs a grainline. Grainlines on a template indicate how to place the template on the fabric when marking so that the threads, or grain, of the fabric are aligned with as many straight edges of the template as possible. Since most of these pieces are curved, it is quite possible that all the edges will be on the bias (not on the straight of grain), no matter how you position the template on the fabric, so being overly concerned with grainlines for this reason is superfluous.

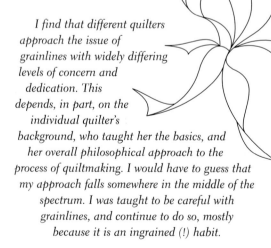

*I find that different quilters approach the issue of grainlines with widely differing levels of concern and dedication. This depends, in part, on the individual quilter's background, who taught her the basics, and her overall philosophical approach to the process of quiltmaking. I would have to guess that my approach falls somewhere in the middle of the spectrum. I was taught to be careful with grainlines, and continue to do so, mostly because it is an ingrained (!) habit.*

I do, however, feel that the grain of some fabrics is very visible, and if that is the case, the pieces need to be placed carefully so that the grain will be consistent in each piece. It is also important that the pieces on the outer edges of the quilt are cut on the straight of grain so that the edges don't stretch. I place all grainlines running vertically, and I put an arrow only on the top end of the line, as in Illustration 3-21 on page 78. This indicates not only which way the grain of the fabric should go, but also which end of the template is toward the top. Therefore, I can tell at a glance which end of the template goes toward the top of the quilt and position it on the fabric accordingly.

## Registration Marks

The next markings I add to the master pattern are registration marks. These marks are similar to the notches used in dressmaking patterns and, in this case, are little slash lines that sit perpendicular to the curved seamlines, as shown on the two templates in 3-22A. When two templates are cut apart, half of the slash will be on one template, the other half on the second template (3-22B). These marks are then transferred to the seam allowance on the back of the fabric (3-22 C and D), and subsequently aligned when the two pieces of fabric are pinned prior to sewing, as shown in 3-22E. Aligning these marks ensures that the fullness of the curve is eased in the proper place, thus ensuring that the seam will lie flat after sewing and pressing. The registration marks should be placed quite close together when the curve is sharp, probably every ¼" or ½". They can be spaced further apart when the curve is more gradual, and eliminated altogether on straight seams.

3-22 A    Templates still joined

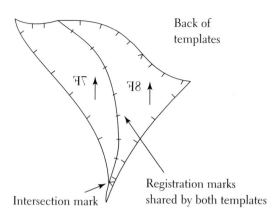

Back of
templates

7F

8F

Intersection mark

Registration marks
shared by both templates

3-22 B    Templates cut apart

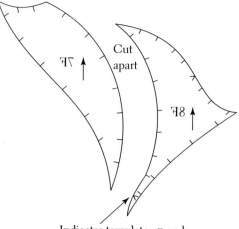

7F

Cut
apart

8F

Indicates template 7F ends
here, not at end of template 8F

3-22 C    Transfer marks from templates to fabric

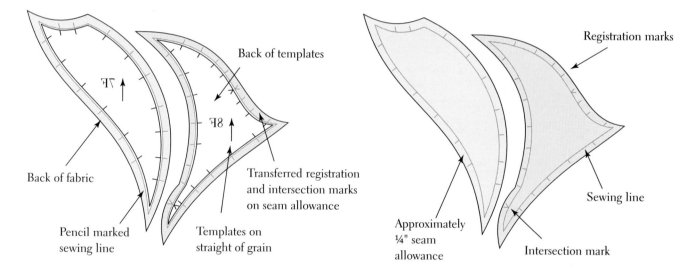

7F

Back of templates

8F

Back of fabric

Transferred registration
and intersection marks
on seam allowance

Pencil marked
sewing line

Templates on
straight of grain

3-22 D    Back of fabric with markings

Registration marks

Approximately
¼" seam
allowance

Sewing line

Intersection mark

3-22 E    Match registration marks. Bring end of seamline on 7F to
          intersection mark on 8F (not end of seamline). 7F is shorter.

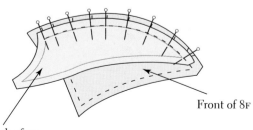

Front of 8F

Back of 7F

MORNING THROUGH THE MIST, 1986
64" x 42", *Judy B. Dales*

The design for this quilt was inspired by an early morning view
of the small town in Vermont where I grew up. Photo: *Young
Masters Studio*

*I designate letters
and numbers
to templates arbitrarily,
in a sequence that
means something to
me. Occasionally,
students assume that my
numbering system refers
to piecing order, but I
assure you it does not! I do not
have the powers of
concentration to plot the
entire piecing order in advance!
I usually just plan three of four
steps ahead when I'm
piecing and hope for
the best!*

If you are working on a Kaleidomosaic or a repeat block design, don't forget to add intersection marks to the outer edges of the blocks or wedges. You may need to trace off a portion of the design in order to do this, but having the marks will be very helpful when the wedges or blocks are sewn together.

Feel free to add any other information to the pattern at this point. You might wish to indicate where you will use dark or light fabrics, or a few small arrows might indicate which way a template should be placed on a directional fabric, such as a stripe or plaid, to enhance the design.

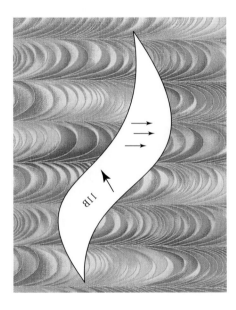

3-26

*I learned to keep the master pattern intact the hard way with my first curved-seam design, America, the Beautiful (page 7). I merrily cut up the pattern to use as templates, only to discover that assembling the quilt was as challenging as doing a jigsaw puzzle, only I didn't even have a picture on the box top to refer to!! You may think that your small drawing will be enough of a piecing guide, but trust me, it isn't!*

## Don't Cut It Up!

The drawing that you have just created, complete with all the markings, is the master pattern. It contains very important information, and ***it will not be cut up*** because you will need to refer to it many times during the making of the quilt top. It will tell you exactly how one piece fits with its neighbor, if you are trying to sew a piece on upside down, how many registration marks should be between two points, and other valuable information.

SPIRIT FLIGHT, 1993
53" x 73", *Judy B. Dales*

This quilt is part of The White House Permanent Craft Collection, assembled by
President and Mrs. Clinton in 1993 to celebrate The Year of The American Craft. The
quilt is dedicated to my mother, Narcissa Cameron Boyd, who was a great admirer of
quilts, and my biggest fan, even though (or perhaps because) she could hardly sew on a
button! Photo: *The Photographic House, Inc.*

# Templates

## Template Material

I make templates by tracing the master pattern and pasting the tracing to lightweight poster board, or tag board. I use poster board because it is relatively inexpensive, comes in fairly large sheets, and is easy to cut (even though it is fairly stiff). Often, a curved-seam design will require a template for every piece in the finished quilt. This means that there needs to be a sheet of template material as large as the actual quilt. Not only would that much template plastic be very expensive, but it can also be difficult to cut with scissors if it is good sturdy plastic. It is also important to know which side of the template is the front, and my method of making templates makes this clear and reverses the pattern in the process.

## Tricky Maneuvers

Because the line that is marked is the sewing line, it needs to be done on the back of the fabric. Therefore, the pattern needs to be reversed at some point so that the finished quilt will not be a mirror image of the master pattern. In some cases, this might not be a problem, but it could be a disaster if the design is directional, as was the case with my quilt, *West With the Night* (page 67). Because of the title, it was imperative that the birds were flying in the same direction as on the master pattern. Reversing the pattern during the template-making process accomplished this quite nicely.

It is customary today to add a ¼" seam allowance to all the templates in a design, which allows quick cutting techniques to be used, and/or the opportunity to mark the cutting line, which can be done on either the front or back of the fabric. However, for curves I've discovered it is better to make the templates the finished size of the piece, without the addition of the ¼" seam allowance. This avoids the tedious task of adding the ¼" seam allowance to all of the numerous templates required. It also allows the marking of the sewing line, which ensures greater accuracy when piecing, and allows the transference of the registration marks and intersection marks to the seam allowance area on the back of the fabric.

It would be ideal if the sewing line could be marked on the back of the fabric, and the seam allowance were also a perfect ¼", but if it is necessary to choose between the two, I opt for marking the sewing line. I cut the fabric pieces ¼" bigger than the marked line, being as accurate as I can manage, just by "eye-balling" it. Fortunately, it is irrelevant whether the seam allowance is perfectly accurate or not, because we will be matching the two drawn sewing lines when we pin and sew, not the edges of the fabric.

## Trace the Master Pattern

To make templates, find a piece of tracing paper that is at least as big as your master pattern. Art supply stores and good stationery stores sell 36"- or 48"- wide tracing paper on a roll, which is ideal for this. Occasionally, two lengths will need to be taped together to achieve the proper size.

Everything on the master pattern needs to be transferred carefully and accurately to the tracing, including grainlines, template labels, registration marks, and intersection marks. Make sure that you copy everything exactly so that what appears on your templates will be the exact duplicate of the information on your master pattern. This will be helpful in the sewing stage when you might wish to know exactly how many registration marks there should be on a particular seam, or if you need to check exactly where a point ends.

The tracing can be done with a pencil or a fine marker, but the line needs to be relatively thin so that there is no ambiguity when the templates are cut apart. A wide line can give you more latitude than is desirable. The lines and marks also need to be dark enough that you can see them from the back of the tracing, so whatever you use, make sure it is visible from the reverse side.

At this point, be careful to put intersection marks exactly at the end of the points. If the lines are thick, there can be ¹⁄₁₆" difference between the inner part of the actual point and the outer point due to that thickness. Put the intersection mark at the exact end of the point, and when you cut the templates, make sure that you cut exactly as marked. Inaccuracies at intersections can "pinch" the work, meaning the top will be distorted at every intersection. This multiplies greatly over the entire top and can be a disaster.

3-25A

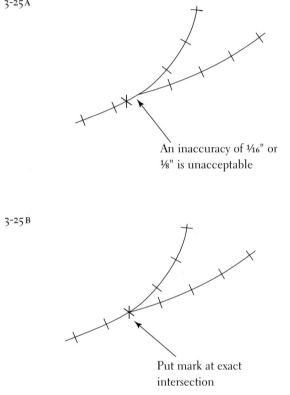

An inaccuracy of ¹⁄₁₆" or ¹⁄₈" is unacceptable

3-25B

Put mark at exact intersection

## Prepare the Poster Board

When the tracing is complete, prepare a piece of poster board, making it a few inches bigger than the tracing. If it is necessary to join several pieces together, butt the edges together and use masking tape to secure them. Luckily, most poster board seems to be cut very accurately, so they usually fit together nicely. Some poster board is shiny on one side, dull on the other. If so, put the tape on the dull side of the poster board. The tracing will be glued to the shiny side, so all joints will have paper on one side and tape on the other, which makes for a strong, stable joining.

## Apply the Adhesive

I recommend using repositionable spray adhesive to adhere the tracing paper to the poster board. Find a clean, flat surface on which to work, in a place with good ventilation. Protect the surrounding surface from overspray, and try to breathe as little of the vapor as possible. Working outdoors is a good idea, but avoid windy or very cold days, as the wind can blow the spray, and extreme cold affects its performance. I have found 3M Artist's Spray Mount® to be the brand I like the best because it gives good, even coverage, but I'm sure there are other good brands.

Lay the poster board dull side down, so that the shiny side is facing up. Spray it evenly with the adhesive, making sure to cover the entire surface. It's important to shake the can repeatedly, because all the good sticky stuff seems to be at the bottom of the can. After the glue dries (about 30 seconds), the entire surface should be tacky. Test with your fingers and respray any areas that you missed. Once the glue is dry, it seems to be inert so it doesn't transfer to other surfaces.

## Stick It

The tracing is now ready to be attached to the poster board, and here comes the tricky part! The *front* of the tracing will be adhered to the poster board, not the back, as would normally be the case. This may seem strange, but this is the step that reverses the whole pattern. More importantly, this maneuver positions the registration and intersection marks on the back of the templates, where they need to be.

Remember that because you are marking the sewing line, rather than the cutting line, the marking must be done on the back of the fabric, so that when the two pieces of fabric are put right sides together, the marks will be visible. Therefore, the fabric will be positioned for marking and cutting with the right, or front side down, and the wrong, or back side facing up. The template will be positioned so that it is facing the same way as the fabric (front side down), with the back side up and the markings showing. Not only does this allow you to see all the marks, but it ensures that the quilt will turn out exactly as the master pattern, with no reversal. By gluing the tracing onto the poster board "backwards," you are making the necessary reversal and positioning the registration and intersection marks so that they can be seen.

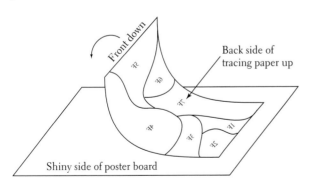

3-26    Smooth out wrinkles

*If you didn't actually understand this explanation, don't worry! It will become clear to you when you actually begin to use the templates. The one quirk of this method is that it will reverse all the writing and letters. I have found that this doesn't bother me in the least. I must be dyslexic, because I can read the numbers backwards as well as frontwards. However, if you suspect it will be a problem for you, rewrite the numbers properly on the back of the template (with all the other information) in a different color pen. Don't write anything on the front of the template because this will be confusing when you start to use them. The thing to remember is that the front of the template is the blank side, and the back has the markings!*

If you are working on a very large piece, you might want to cut the templates into several large sections at this point. I wouldn't, however, cut them all apart. Having them all separated in advance just means that you will need to search for each one individually when you need it. If the templates are still intact, you can just cut each one away as you need it, use it, then lay it aside when you are finished.

I know you are probably thinking that this is a lot of rigmarole just to make a quilt pattern, and I agree that it seems quite daunting. However, I have discovered that many of the more exciting and challenging things in life do require careful, tedious preparation procedures. I personally feel that curved seams are worth all the extra effort, and I hope you will too. Keep in mind that by the time you get to this stage, you've done most of the boring stuff and now comes the fun part. Fabric!!

Chapter Four

# Finally, The Fabric!

THE START, 1991
30" x 24", *Judy B. Dales*

Created as a twenty-fifth anniversary present for my husband,
who is an avid sailor, this small wallhanging is based on a
painting by Charles Sheeler. Collection of G. *Anders Dales.*
Photo: *Ricardo Barras*

# Fabric Interpretation

## Using a Design Wall

I think it is essential to make all fabric choices before doing any sewing, and it's a good idea to let the design "rest" on the design wall for a day or two before beginning to actually stitch. If you have the luxury of a few extra days, you can then return with fresh eyes and sensibilities, and often will see things that escaped you before, or things that need to be changed. I also find that color combinations look different depending on the available light. Not only do I avoid making color choices at night because it is hard to work with color in artificial light, but I also like to view the design on different days, or at the very least, different times of day. It's amazing how the colors change with different types of light, and how much the natural light changes from morning to evening.

## Fabric Choices

Choosing fabrics can be the most challenging and frustrating part of the design process, but also the most fun. Individual approaches to designing vary a great deal, but I feel that those who approach it with a spirit of adventure and play are often more successful and enjoy the process more than the serious, intent designer.

Don't attempt to preplan the whole project before one piece of fabric is cut. I understand that fabric is precious, and that none of us want to waste any, but unfortunately, wasting a little fabric is an inevitable part of the process. Cutting a specific piece and placing it in the design will tell you almost immediately if that fabric is right or not, while staring at a yard and a half of the same fabric for two hours will tell you almost nothing.

If I have to discard a piece of fabric because it isn't working, I remind myself that I would rather waste a few bits of fabric than waste months of my time working on a quilt that has a major "indiscretion." If a fabric choice bothers you during the design process, you can be sure it will still bother you when the quilt is finished, probably even more. So change it now, and don't hesitate to spend the time and effort necessary to get it right at this stage.

Every scrap of fabric is precious, so it is all saved for later use. Rejected pieces are stored with the pattern in case the design is used again. I keep random scraps in a basket, and it's amazing that all of them eventually get used. Long skinny strips make fabric balls, which are totally useless but charming!

## Color, Value, and Texture

The three elements inherent in printed fabric are color, value, and texture; the challenge is to manipulate these three elements in order to create contrasts. Contrast is a key component of quilt design and it is contrast that will separate, highlight, and distinguish various parts of the design and direct the eye of the viewer.

I have used the same fabric for each piece in the block below (4-1), so there is no color change, value change, or texture change, and therefore no contrast. It seems elementary, but it's amazing how often we don't think about creating contrast.

4-1    No contrast

In an attempt to mentally sort out the roles value, color, and texture play in the design process, it can be helpful to create a block using each in isolation. Figure 4-2 shows a block using only color contrast: the fabrics are all the same light value and the exact same print, so there is no value or texture contrast. The block is not effective because there is so little definition that the star motif is almost completely obscured. Is this an indication that color is actually not very important in the design process?

The block in 4-3 was interpreted using only value contrast. Different values in the same color family were used, and the prints are all hand-dyed, so there is no color contrast or texture contrast. This block is a bit better than the color block, only because the star is well defined and there is sharp contrast between foreground and background, but the lack of texture and color contrast creates a very boring block.

Figure 4-4 is a block created using only texture contrast (different prints). The color and value of each of the fabrics is the same, so color and value contrast play very little part in the design. This is actually quite a good interpretation. The block is reasonably well defined, there is good contrast between foreground and background, and it is more interesting than the other two. Obviously visual texture plays a vital role in the design process.

In 4-5, all three elements have been used in combination to produce a stunning block. The value contrast defines the design, the good visual texture ensures that all areas of the design are interesting, and the colors are lush. Notice that the colors were chosen with no regard to whether they "matched." Excitement, impact, and interest are the function of colors in a quilt, and those goals will rarely be accomplished with fabrics that "match."

4-2 Color contrast

4-3 Value contrast

4-4 Texture contrast

4-5 Good color, value, and texture contrast

Most quilters tend to agonize over color, but most often the difficulties encountered in quilt design are problems with value or texture, not color. Color choices should be intuitive, based on emotions and feelings, because color preferences are a result of our own individual life experience. Most of us just need to be convinced that our color choices are valid, and we need to develop enough confidence to trust our own instincts. Because our color preferences are so personal and subjective, the colors one person uses may be very different from another person's. Who is to say one is right and the other wrong?

4-6 The fabrics shown here are similar in value and texture. They were chosen to show color contrast.

In the Pink, 1986
60" x 52", *Judy B. Dales*

Although I love this quilt because pink is my favorite color, I have to admit that it
suffers greatly from a lack of value contrast. I went through a period where my value
contrasts became so subtle, they were almost nonexistent. I have to continually
remind myself to pay more attention to value contrast.

In my own mind, I've decided that color rules and theory are too intellectual for me, and I prefer to take a more spontaneous, intuitive approach. The first suggestion I would give is, if you like it, use it. I have never understood why quilters sometimes feel compelled to use colors they dislike intensely. Why should you use colors you don't like?

I grant you that there are times when an "ugly" fabric or color is just the right thing to perk up a dull palette, or that you might want to use colors you dislike in order to express some specific, perhaps negative, emotion. But I can't understand why you would choose to work with colors that don't appeal to you. I think making a quilt should be a joyful and satisfying experience, and the colors you work with should make your heart sing and your soul happy.

Over the years, I have learned to like a few colors that I previously disliked intensely, so it is quite possible for one's opinions to change. I suspect that appreciation for the way those colors behave in someone else's quilt has affected my opinion, and I have begun to incorporate them into my palette. But the change has occurred gradually, and I have never tried to facilitate it by forcing myself to work in those colors.

So, how do you tell if you "like" a certain colored fabric? Well, you cut a piece, put it on the design wall with your other fabric choices, and see what happens. Does it do what you had hoped? Does it work well with the other fabrics you've chosen? Does it do its part, whatever you want that part to be? If not, try another.

To answer the question "Do these two fabrics 'go' together?", put them together and see how you like the combination. Will this shade of purple be happy next to that shade of green? Try it and see! You will probably know immediately if it's wrong, and can try another combination. If you are undecided, it's probably not a color issue. If a fabric doesn't behave the way you thought it would, it's probably because of its value or texture, not its color. I am not advocating thoughtless quilt designing. I am simply recommending that you think very hard about value and texture, but respond on a more intuitive level to color.

The elements of value and texture need to be subjected to a rigorous and analytical evaluation. Value is often the backbone of a quilt design, and the contrasts between light, medium, and dark values are usually what defines the design and distinguishes foreground from background. These fabrics below show value contrast. They range from very light, through medium, to very dark.

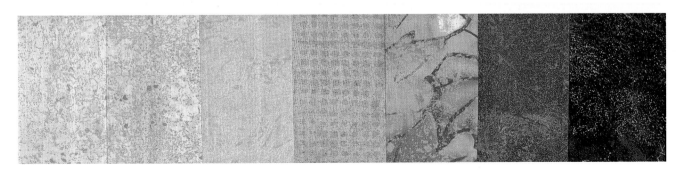

4-7   Very light to very dark value contrast.

4-8  What value is it?     4-9  Now it is lighter.     4-10  Now it is darker.

4-11  Is it a Medium?

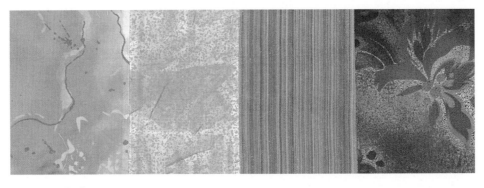

4-12  It's a Dark!

4-13  It's a Light!

It would be difficult, if not impossible, to give a value label to the fabric in 4-8 because value is a relative concept. Is it a Light, a Medium, or a Dark? The proper answer is "I don't know." In 4-9, it is quite easy to see that the original fabric is lighter than its companion, and in 4-10, it is darker. Because we know that our fabric sample is darker than some fabrics and lighter than others, it would be logical to assume that it is a Medium and, in fact, it works quite nicely as a Medium in the value range in 4-11.

However, look what happens if all the darker fabrics are taken away from the combination, as in 4-12. Now our Medium is acting like a Dark. It is not very dark, but in this combination, it is darker than its companions, so we label it a Dark. The opposite is true in 4-13. Here all the lighter fabrics have been removed, so in this combination, our sample fabric is behaving like the Light. Any fabric can behave as a Light, a Medium, or a Dark, depending what fabrics they are combined with.

The third element, texture, is the visual effect created by the different types of patterns printed on the fabric, and it is the effective use of this element that will play a powerful role in the creation of a dazzling quilt. Visual texture is created by a number of factors, among which are the size (or scale), of the print, the type of print, the arrangement of the print on the surface of the fabric, and an elusive element that I think of as the "personality" of the print.

The fabrics below are all in the same value range and the same color family. It is the contrast between the different visual textures created by the print that enables you to distinguish one from the other.

4-14 Visual texture contrast

4-15  Type of print

The type of print is probably the first thing you notice when you look at a fabric, and the variety of types available is astounding: stripes, plaids, paisley, florals, abstracts, watercolor, hand-dyed crystals, and many more that have no names (4-15).

The second aspect of the prints we think about is the size, or scale of the print. Even though these two fabrics are quite similar to each other, they actually look very different because of their scale (4-16).

The density of a print affects its visual texture. When cut into small pieces, a compact, dense print will behave completely differently than a loose print with a lot of background area (4-17).

But it is the combination of all these elements that creates the effect of personality, and this is what makes fabric so appealing to us. When we fall in love with a fabric, it is the personality that we are responding to. Sometime, listen to your quilt friends describing a piece of fabric. They may call it cute, beautiful, elegant, cool, or ugly. These signals that emote from the various prints can be a powerful tool in quiltmaking and will help determine the message your quilt delivers and how people respond to it.

One of the prints shown below (4-18) is full of energy and reminds me of a hyperactive thirteen-year-old. The other is exotic and mysterious. The personality of prints is a powerful element, and being sensitive to it can add a great deal to our quilts.

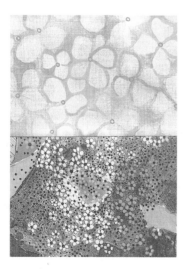

4-16  Scale of print

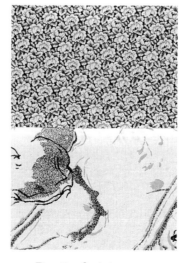

4-17  Density of print

4-18  Personality of print

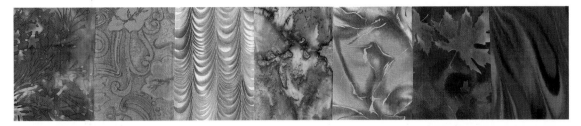

4-19   Fabrics that enhance curves

4-20   Fabrics that interfere with curves

## Enhancing Curves with Textures

Particular attention needs to be given to the visual texture of fabrics to be used with curves. A great deal of work has gone into producing a design with flow and grace, so the fabric needs to enhance this flow, not detract from it. Look for prints with a flowing, sophisticated feel to them: abstract watercolors designs, curved prints, fabric with gradual color changes, and flowing lines that will add to the feeling of movement (4-19).

Avoid geometrics, novelty prints, and other hard-edged, regimented designs that will interfere with the fluid feel of your design (4-20).

## Background Areas

It is important to pay special attention to the background area of your quilt, because not only does it help to determine the whole mood of the piece, it can often be one-third of the total surface of the quilt. The colors and textures should be subtle, not too high contrast, and multi-colored, which will help pull together all the diverse colors in the main part of the quilt. The print needs to be interesting enough that it can fill the large expanse of background effectively, but not so busy or strong that it will overwhelm the central design.

I often use ten or more different prints in the background, but I am careful to choose fabrics that read the same and will stay in the background. It was my search for good light-value background fabrics that led me to the decorator department of the fabric store. In fact, most of the fabrics shown below (4-21) are home decorating fabrics.

4-21  Appropriate background fabrics

## Problem Solving

Occasionally, in the design process, I will encounter one specific piece that gives me a significant amount of trouble, and it usually ends up being the very last choice to be made. Unfortunately, it is often a large piece also, which means I waste a lot of fabric trying to find the best choice. After trying every conceivable choice, I may decide that the problem is not with the fabric, but is actually a problem with the design. Perhaps the piece is too large, or it may be an awkward shape that draws the eye to it. Fortunately, the design can still be altered at this point. A large shape can be divided by simply drawing a new seamline directly on the front of the template. Cut the two pieces apart, then flip them over, realign the pieces, and add the registration and intersection marks on the back.

Conversely, small pieces can be joined by simply taping the templates together, and seamlines that don't appeal can be altered by taping all the involved templates together securely, redrawing the seam, and cutting it differently. It's comforting to know that things can be changed, even at this stage of the game. Don't forget to make corresponding notations on the master pattern, eliminating or adding intersection marks to adjacent templates, if necessary, to reflect these changes.

When I am approaching the selection of fabric for a quilt, I usually have only a very vague notion of what colors I want to use, and may have pulled a grouping from my stash to start with, but I am usually pretty certain of the value placement. In fact, I may do a gray-scale sketch of the design in which I use a regular lead pencil, varying the pressure and density of lines to produce darker and lighter areas in the design. Then as I begin to cut, at least I know when to choose a Light, Medium, or Dark, or where I want the value contrasts to fall. Other fabrics are incorporated as the design process progresses. Notice in the photo above that the numbers and letters are reversed on the back of the templates, which is correct.

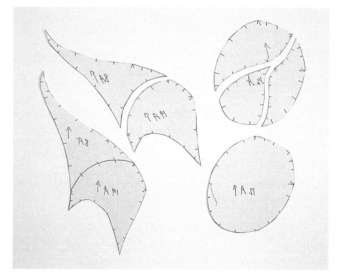

## The Right Attitude

One advantage to approaching fabric choices with an open mind and a willingness to experiment is that you can come up with some amazingly effective and different combinations. People often comment on my unusual fabric choices, and I hear again and again, "I would never have thought to put those two fabrics together." I find that an interesting turn of phrase! I probably wouldn't have "thought" to put those fabrics together either, but in the process of rummaging through my stash and trying practically every piece that fell to hand, I did try those two particular fabrics together! The combination may be unusual, effective, and just what I was looking for, but it was the result of experimentation rather than deliberate thought. I firmly believe that designing is a process of doing, not necessarily one of thinking. So don't agonize or ponder too long—just try the piece and see how it looks.

It takes a certain amount of courage and risk-taking to be a good quilt designer. Safe and conservative fabric choices may save you from a total failure, but it could also prevent the creation of something wonderful. There are several important things to keep in mind when choosing fabric for your quilt design that might help you be more adventurous with your choices.

First of all, remember that you are designing a quilt, not decorating your home or putting together an outfit to wear. The rules of the latter two don't apply because the goal in quiltmaking is entirely different than those of fashion or interior design. In fashion, we seek coordinated combinations that will create a pleasing cover for the body, but nothing so dramatic that it will overwhelm the person herself. The decorating scheme of a room should be merely a backdrop for the living that will take place there. However, in quiltmaking, the quilt is not the backdrop for anything. The quilt is the primary focus, and as such may require more than a simple, coordinated color scheme. It requires a design and coloration that have impact, make a statement, draw the viewer in, and/or shout to the world, "Look at me!" In order to achieve that effect, "aim for awesome" when you are making fabric choices, and don't be timid!

## Make It Yours

Keep in mind that this quilt is your creation, and, as such, should reflect your choices and your personal preferences. Only you hold the inner vision of how you want your quilt to look, so only you can really make the fabric choices that will express your ideas and make the statement you want them to make.

## Know When To Quit

Hopefully, you will reach a point in the design process when all the major challenges have been resolved, the whole design looks good, and you can sigh contentedly and decide that it is time to sew. However, some quilt projects never seem to reach this point conclusively. You can, of course, prolong the design process as long as you've a mind to, but the quest for design perfection is probably the quilter's biggest saboteur. The quilter who expects and demands that the design be perfect will probably never sew it together, because, of course, the design will never be absolutely, one hundred percent perfect. Nothing ever is!

*I find that there comes a time with every project when I have just had enough. Perhaps it's really just impatience, or lack of perseverance, but I have no desire to turn a quilt project into an endurance test. I become eager to move on, partly because I want to see the top sewn together (it always looks significantly better after it's sewn), and partly because I'm already looking forward to the next project.*

However you manage it, bring the design process to closure. Give yourself a time limit, set a deadline, ask a friend to nudge you forward, but somehow, get on with it. It may be comforting to know that all artists face this dilemma. The filmmaker must eventually decide that he's done enough takes, the potter must finally commit the pot to the oven. It may help to remind yourself that the primary goal is making quilts, not torturing yourself with agonizing, endless design decisions. Finish this quilt so that you can carry forward to the next project the knowledge that this one has given you.

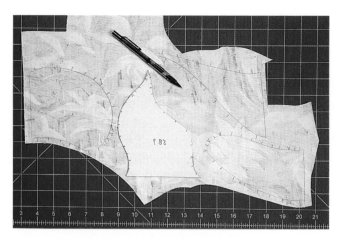

Fabric and template back (wrong) side up

## Marking and Cutting
### Preparation

I cut out all the pieces and put them on the design wall before I begin any of the sewing. I want to be certain that I'm happy with each and every fabric choice before I proceed. It is difficult to make the design look tidy at this stage because each piece is bigger than it will be when it's actually sewn, and nothing seems to fit together. Just overlap them a little to make them fit as well as possible.

I cut each template as I use it, and then lay it aside when I am finished. Before I mark and cut, I press the fabric. Not only do wrinkles and creases distort the fabric, but the individual pieces tend not to stay on the design wall very well if they are creased.

The fabric is placed right side down onto my green cutting mat, which I find has just enough roughness to prevent the fabric from sliding around as I do the marking. The template goes onto the back of the fabric, front side down and back side up, so that the marks are visible. Remember that the back side of the template has the marks on it, including reversed numbers and letters, and the front side is blank. If you cannot see the marks, you know you've put the template down wrong.

### Template Positioning

Remember that you are going to cut the pieces of fabric ¼" bigger than the template, so you have to allow for this when you place the template on the back of the fabric. Avoid placing a template too close to any edges, especially the selvage edge, and when you are cutting two pieces side-by-side, leave at least a ½" between them, a ¼" seam allowance for each piece.

The template should be positioned so that the mark for the grainline runs parallel to either the lengthwise or crosswise grain of the fabric, in line with the threads. However, if you wish to take advantage of a particular area of the printed design, the template can be positioned off-grain. The grainlines are more important visually than technically when working with curves, since all the edges are bias anyway. So if the piece looks better positioned off-grain, don't hesitate to use it that way.

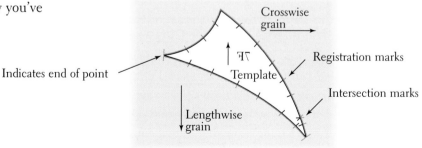

Indicates end of point

Crosswise grain

Template

Registration marks

Intersection marks

Lengthwise grain

4-22 Wrong side of fabric

ALASKA QUILT, 1997
43" x 38", *Judy B. Dales*

I was lucky enough to go with Doreen Speckmann on one of her quilters' cruises through Alaska and thought the occasion warranted a new quilt. See the Eagle project on page 148.

## Marking Tools

When the template is positioned where you want it, mark carefully all around it, making sure to angle the pencil in toward the template to get the line as close as possible. Also be sure that you are using either a fine-lead mechanical pencil, or a very well-sharpened regular pencil. I use a mechanical pencil with a 0.7mm lead, which is a little thicker than the 0.5mm so that it doesn't break as readily, and the line is easier to see than that made by a finer lead.

Finding a marker that you can see is critical. Often, if you work at it, you can see regular lead on even the darkest fabrics, because it has a bit of a shine that you can detect as you move the fabric at different angles. Keep a pencil sharpener nearby because you will need to sharpen the lead before practically every line you draw. However, if you need a different marker for dark fabrics, try a silver pencil. If the back of the fabric has a gray coloration, even the silver marker is hard to see, so I will occasionally use colored pencils in a complementary color, so that the line will be visible. Do be sure to test to see that the colored pencil will either wash out completely when you launder your quilt, or remain totally permanent, and that the pencil line doesn't bleed through to the front side of the fabric.

Keep in mind that if you use a mechanical pencil for marking some of the pieces and a regular or colored pencil for others, you will have to compensate for the difference in the thickness of the two lines somewhere in the sewing process. When I pin two pieces with different lines, I compensate for this discrepancy by placing the pin slightly below the colored pencil line to adjust for the added thickness.

Quilters are often tempted to use a fine-tip felt marker, but if the mark is truly permanent, it may show through to the right side of the fabric where your stitching is not perfect. On the other hand, if the marker washes out completely and you plan to launder your quilt, a marker could be perfectly suitable. Do not use a wash-out blue marker, because the pressing of each seam that is necessary during the sewing process will make it permanent. Be very sure in your mind about how the finished product will be cared for and choose the appropriate tool, but be sure to test all markers before you begin!

As you mark the sewing line, be sure not to drag your pencil too hard, which will stretch and distort the fabric. Keep one hand firmly on the template so it doesn't shift, and use light, feathery strokes to draw the line. Go over it several times if it is not dark enough. Pay particular attention to skinny points, making sure that you don't bend the template. As added insurance, I make a mark perpendicular to a long, sharp point that indicates exactly where the point ends. This way, if my lines don't quite meet at the tip, I will still know where the point should end. After you have marked the sewing line, mark all the registration marks and intersection marks in the seam allowance as shown. Be sure that these are very accurate and quite visible. They will be very important later. See the illustration (4-22) on page 100.

## Rotary Cutter for Curves

Curves can be cut with scissors, which I did for years, but I have discovered that it is much faster to use a rotary cutter. I use a cutter with a small blade and carefully cut ¼" outside the drawn line. This can seem pretty scary the first time you try it, but becomes quite easy with practice. Cut very slowly and carefully, being sure to keep your fingers out of the way. Try not to be overly generous with your ¼" seam allowance. In fact, aim for a scant ¼", because if you are too generous, you will find yourself trimming the seam allowance when you get to the pinning stage. Curves need to be flexible so that you can bend one piece of fabric around to line up with another. If the seam allowance is too wide, you lose the flexibility, and that makes easing very difficult.

Certain angles and directions can be very awkward to cut, so occasionally I will cut a shape roughly first. Then the fabric can be shifted to give you a better angle without having to maneuver two or three yards of fabric, and the piece can be cut more accurately. In fact, sometimes I move the fabric simultaneously as I cut to help get around a sharp curve. This takes some practice, but once you feel confident with the rotary cutter, you will find your own methods.

Since only one layer is being cut and there is no ruler to press against, it is not necessary to bear down terribly hard with the cutter, especially if it is good and sharp, so I find that I can do the cutting sitting down. I have a secretary's chair that can be adjusted up or down, which allows me to sit high enough to see what I am doing.

One of the hardest things to control when using a rotary cutter is the exact place where a cut ends. Care must be taken not to cut too far into "virgin" fabric at the end of points, and at angles or you will waste fabric, or worse yet, discover a little cut in a subsequent piece. Stop as accurately as you can, and cut off the excess fabric at the end of a skinny tip, as it is not important and will only have to be trimmed later.

Rotary cutting curves

Chapter Five
# Getting It Together

Fantasy Form #341, 1996
34" x 45", *Judy B. Dales*

This quilt is the second in my Fantasy Form series. The watercolor effect is created by overlays of tulle and chiffon, but the major portion of the design is pieced.

# Before You Stitch

## Sewing Sequence

Sewing order is probably one of the most intimidating challenges with curve-seam piecing. To a novice, there just doesn't seem to be any logical order or obvious place to start, and there certainly can be an awesome array of pieces. The best advice I can offer is that you refuse to be intimidated by the amount of work that looms before you. Just tackle it one seam at a time! Many quilters seem to want to know exactly how they are going to proceed, but figuring it all out ahead of time is a daunting task, one that could discourage even the most determined sewer. Just pick an obvious place to start and begin. You might work from the center out, from top to bottom, or, if there are obvious units, begin with those. In our small demo quilt (5-1), I would probably start with the pieces forming the abstract flower shape. In Illustration 5-2, the red numbers show the sewing sequence.

Quite often, the logical sewing sequence is not the most obvious one, or the one that you would instinctively choose. For example, with this small design, you might be inspired to sew the entire flower form together and then add in the background, but that would force you to set some of the background pieces into the sharp angles and curves of the flower. Furthermore, if you sew 3F and 4F together, it would be extremely difficult to add 5F because the tiny part of 3F that extends past 4F creates a set-in situation when adding 5F. A better sequence would be to sew 4F and 3B together, then add 5F, followed by 3F and 8F.

While it is not terribly helpful to plot the entire sewing sequence in advance, you do need to plan one or two steps ahead so that you can avoid any problematic situations. In most cases, if you plan three steps ahead that should be enough, but keep in mind that you may not always be sewing the next adjacent pieces together. You may have to jump around, as was necessary in the example.

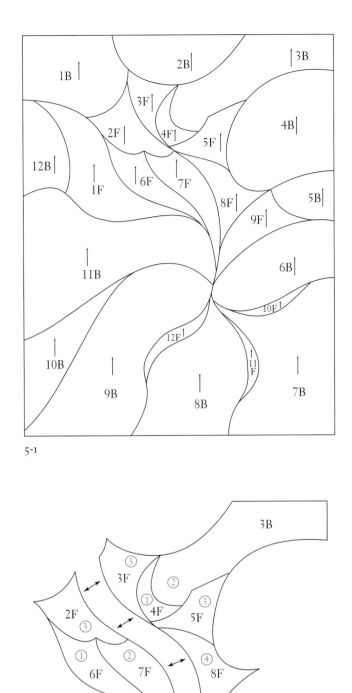

5-1

5-2   Red numbers = sewing sequence

## Hand Versus Machine

The marking, cutting, and pinning procedure is the same whether you sew the actual seam by hand or machine. Because I had been hand sewing for many years before I started doing curves, I always felt more comfortable sewing challenging seams by hand, including curves. However, I have now done so much on the machine that I am completely comfortable with either method.

I used to be a purist, thinking that if I started a project by hand, I should do the whole thing that way and vice versa. Now I often switch back and forth between the two, depending on the availability of a machine and electricity, and have had no problems combining the two methods. Choose whichever is most comfortable for you.

## Pinning

By far the most time consuming part of the assembly process is the pinning, and the procedure is the same whether you will sew by hand or machine. Good quality pins with a fine shank and medium-sized, glass heads are what I prefer. Make sure you have a good number of them available in a place where they are easy to grab, either a pincushion or a magnetic pin holder.

## Hills and Dales

When aligning two pieces of fabric just prior to pinning, there will be a curve that bumps up (the convex curve, which I call "The Hill"), and the curve that dips down (the concave, which I call "The Dale").

I like to pin from the Hill side, and sew from the Dale side. Begin pinning at either end of the seam, setting the pins perpendicular to the seam. Take care to align the fabric properly at both ends, and then pin in the middle and work your way out to the ends, pinning on each registration mark. Don't yank the fabric around trying to straighten out the seam. It is a curve, and no amount of tugging is going to turn it into a straight line! Rather, coax the Dale piece, which will be sagging down in the back, up so that it curves around the Hill piece. This may take some effort, and the sharper the curve, the harder it may be.

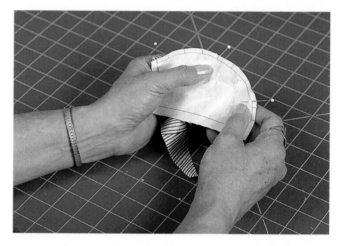

5-5   Pinning and coaxing the Dale up to match the Hill

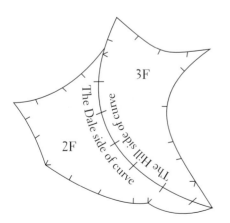

5-3   As seen on the templates

5-4   Hill in front, Dale in back

When the two pieces seem to be aligned, stab the pin exactly through the seamline at a registration mark on the Hill piece, then do the same through the corresponding registration mark on the Dale piece, checking on the back side of the Dale piece to make sure you have done it accurately (5-6). Then squeeze the fabric tightly together, so that you can maneuver the pin down to "take the bite" (5-7). This is one of the tricky parts, so be careful. After having spent all that effort coaxing the Dale piece up to match the Hill, the Dale has a tendency to want to slip back down, and the twisting movement of the pin, if not done carefully, can provide the opportunity for it to do just that. Hold the fabric very tightly together, and maneuver the pin right under the fingers holding the fabric, so that nothing slips. Keep the "bite" short, or, in other words, don't anchor the pin too far below the seamline. If it anchors the fabric in place too far down, it makes easing the rest of the fabric into place a little more difficult.

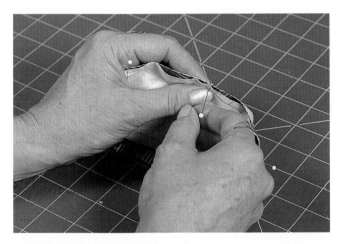

5-6   Pin straight through and check on back

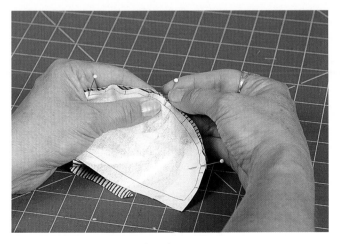

5-7   Maneuvering pin to take a bite

Pin carefully on all the registration marks, and in between, if necessary. A gradual curve will not require nearly as many pins as a sharp one, but when in doubt, use more! It's easier to use more pins than rip out a section of seam that wasn't pinned properly.

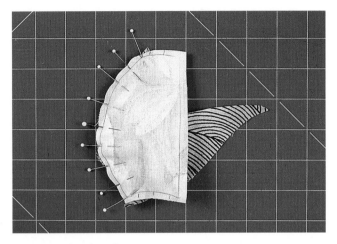

5-8   Pinned and ready to sew

As you pin, you will occasionally have to smooth the fullness of the curve away from the seamline on the Dale side, and occasionally you may have to release a pin to readjust the fullness. Keep checking to make sure that you are pinning exactly on the line on both pieces of fabric. Accurate pinning is essential to accurate piecing.

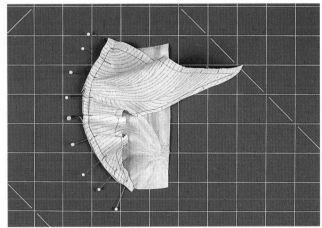

5-9   Readjust fullness if needed

## Break It Down

Occasionally you will encounter long seams that look extremely challenging, with curves that bend first one way, then the other. Don't be intimidated! You can break these seams into smaller sections because the registration marks indicate how to line the seams up, as well as give you very obvious places to stop and start. Pin one section of the curve on the Hill side, then flip the two pieces over so that you can still pin from the Hill side on the next section of curve. If it is a long seam, you may have to flip it back and forth several times so that you can always work on the side that feels the most comfortable.

If you have a great deal of trouble easing two pieces together, check your master pattern to ensure that you aren't trying to do the impossible. If I've been trying to pin two pieces together for more than a few minutes with no success, I can assume that I'm doing something wrong, such as pulling a point further along than it should go, or trying to pin two pieces together that aren't supposed to go together. I've learned that if I've been struggling for fifteen minutes, it's time to check the master pattern!! That's what it's there for!

A very common mistake is the assumption that points always match up with points. If one piece is smaller than another, as is the case here in 5-10, the point of one piece will stop somewhere along the seam (before the point). There should be an intersection mark to indicate this. If you can't get two pieces to fit, check to make sure you are not overlooking an intersection point on one of the seams. If you find that your marks are difficult to see or not accurate enough, don't hesitate to find your templates and remark the pieces. It is essential that the marks be exact and that you can see them.

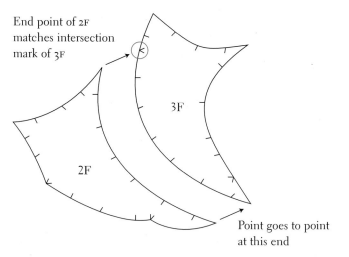

5-10  Check templates for position of intersection marks

End point of 2F matches intersection mark of 3F

Point goes to point at this end

If the seam allowances are too big, the excess fabric outside the seamline will make it difficult to bend the curves around to match each other. Trimming the seam allowances down to an ⅛" will usually encourage the two to line up. If even this doesn't help, I will occasionally do some gentle clipping, but I don't like to do so. I find clipping before sewing can cause the finished seam to have angles in it, rather than a nice smooth curve. Clipping at this point also gives the fabric a chance to fray if you still need to fuss with it, so I only clip before sewing if I'm desperate.

## Stitching
### Hand Sewing

If you choose to sew your curved seams by hand, rest assured that it's not much more time-consuming than machine sewing. Even machines can't go very fast when they are dodging pins and maneuvering around curves! Sometimes it is actually soothing to do hand sewing—there is not nearly the urgency associated with it that sometimes accompanies machine work.

Use a sharp, small needle and a single strand of strong thread with a knot in the end. Use a neutral color, such as beige, gray, or mauve, so that if there is strain on the seam, the thread won't be glaringly obvious. I work with the Hill side toward me, but it really doesn't matter which way you do it, since you can easily check on the back of the work when hand sewing. Try both ways and choose the method that is most comfortable for you.

SEASONS OF THE HEART, 1995
68" diameter, *Judy B. Dales*

This curved Kaleidomosaic design produced a heart motif when the wedges were combined.
Although I am not particularly fond of hearts, I decided to allow these to stay, and chose the title as
a tribute to John Denver and his song of the same name, which is one of my favorites. I always
intended to share a photo of the quilt with him, but unfortunately, I waited too long.

Start the seam at the beginning of the drawn pencil line, not the edge of the fabric, and even though there is a knot in the thread, secure the beginning of the seam with a backstitch for added security. Proceed along the pencil line with a running stitch, taking care to keep the stitches as small as possible, so there will be no gaps in the seam when it is stressed. Take care when you begin to take a new needle full of stitches that you align these stitches carefully with the preceding ones, so that the curve continues smoothly (5-11).

If the seam you are working on crosses an existing seam, don't stitch the seam allowance down. Stitch right up to the seam, and take a backstitch to anchor the stitches. Then slip the needle through the bottom of the seam allowance, and pull it out on the other side of the seam. Stab the needle through both pieces of fabric exactly at the beginning of the seam, and then start stitching again with a backstitch, and continue along the seam. Leaving the seam allowance free allows some flexibility when pressing and also avoids stitching through the bulk of four layers (5-12).

5-11   Hand sewing along penciled seamline

5-12   Leave seam allowance free

It is necessary to check frequently on the back of the work to ensure that the stitches are falling exactly on the pencil line there, as well as on the front piece. Check this before you pull a needle full of stitches through, so that if you need to readjust the needle, it is simply a matter of pulling the needle out and repositioning it. If you check for accuracy after you have pulled the thread through and find that you have missed the line, you will have to unthread the needle, pick out the stitches, and rethread the needle again in order to correct it. This may seem like an insignificant point, but it is one that will save you much time over the course of sewing a complete top.

As you pull the thread through the fabric, don't pull too tightly. Curves need to be flexible and if your thread tension is too tight, you lose that flex. Some teachers recommend a backstitch now and then to strengthen the line of stitching, but I have never felt this was necessary. If your stitches are small enough, the seam should be secure.

When you reach the end of the seam, secure the line of stitching with two backstitches at the end of the marked pencil line. Do not continue to the edge of the fabric. Before you proceed with the clipping and pressing, check on both sides of the seam and on the front of the work to make sure the stitching is accurate and that the curve appears to be smooth, and that there are no pleats or puckers on either side of the seam.

## Machine Sewing

Machine stitching curved seams is actually quite similar to hand sewing. You will be stitching directly on the pencil line, starting and ending the line of stitching exactly at the beginning and end of the line, not the edge of the fabric. I use a neutral colored thread, with normal tension, and a medium stitch length. It is important that the tension on your machine is not too tight, because this will cause puckering and can also eliminate the flex in the seam, which is so important when working with curves. I also take great care in adjusting the stitch length. The stitch needs to be small enough to create a secure seam, but long enough to rip out fairly easily, because there is invariably some ripping that needs to be done! Experiment with your machine a little to discover just the right stitch length and tension.

## Equipment

Curves require very precise sewing, so your machine needs to be working well and have the tension properly adjusted. You also need to be familiar enough with it that you have good control. Some of the newer machines take one extra stitch after you take your foot off the peddle, which can be very disconcerting if you are not accustomed to it. It is essential that you be able to stop and start stitching precisely, so you may need to practice and become familiar with your machine's idiosyncrasies.

I have discovered that the antique Singer Featherweight® is wonderful for sewing curves. This machine has a narrow presser foot and narrow feed dogs, which allow for great maneuverability. Whichever machine you work with, it will need to have a presser foot that is open in the front, so that you can see the pencil line on the fabric and the needle as it is stitching.

Make sure that you are seated comfortably in front of your machine (positioned exactly in front of the needle), and adjust your sitting height so that you don't have to bend over at an awkward angle to see what you are doing. I have an adjustable chair and I keep it set fairly low so that my nose is quite close to my sewing. Good light is, of course, essential, and I find it helpful to have the machine set up reasonably close to the design wall, with an iron also close at hand, so I don't have to be running around the room. However, getting up occasionally is probably not a bad idea either, because long stretches at the sewing machine can be tiring.

## Working with the Dale

Even though we pinned from the Hill side, we are going to machine sew from the Dale side. The piece of fabric on the Dale side is the one with the fullness, and this is where puckers tend to occur. By sewing with this piece on top, you can smooth out the fullness as you go along, avoiding pleats and puckers. Remember that you are sewing a curve. Don't try to force the seam into a straight line. In fact, encourage it to be as curved as it wants by gathering the fabric in your left hand and feeding it into the machine from the side, so that the curve stays nice and curvy (5-13).

5-13 Sewing a curve on the Dale side

Start the seam by putting your needle down exactly at the beginning of the marked line, (not the edge of the fabric). Take two stitches forward, two stitches back, then proceed forward along the marked line. Some sewing machine manufacturers recommend that the seam be anchored by starting off with teeny, tiny stitches. I don't like this suggestion, because the first stitch always seems to pull a bit, no matter how small it is. With my method, the stitch on the end is not the first stitch, so it remains tight.

Stitch slowly and carefully, removing pins just before you get to them. If you are tempted to sew over a pin, you will find that it gets hung up on the feed dogs, so it's just as well to remove it. Slide it out just before the needle gets to it. If you take the pin out too soon, the fabric will slip and your seam won't be accurate. At the end of the seam, backstitch two stitches and clip the threads. Inspect both sides of the seam for puckers and/or places where the stitching missed the line (5-14). The seam may not want to lie flat at this point, but it is better to make stitching corrections before the clipping and pressing stage.

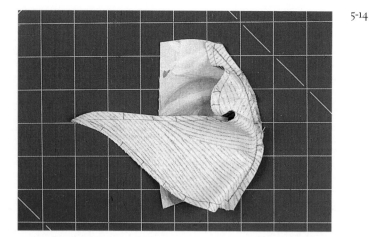

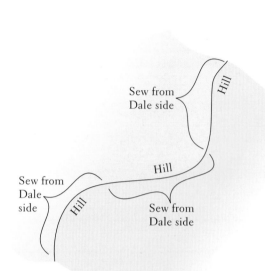

5-15

## Flip It Over

With machine sewing, of course, it is impossible to see what is happening on the underside of the work, which creates unique problems. If you reach a stretch where the curve changes and the Dale is now underneath the Hill, a decision needs to be made. If you continue on, you will need to use your fingers and all your tactile skills to ensure that nothing is bunching or puckering underneath. It is also important to lift up the top layer frequently in order to manipulate the bottom layer and check that things are OK. The alternative is to stop sewing at this point, break the threads, flip the work over, and sew from the other side, overlapping the stitching to secure the seam. Usually this is the better choice, even though it takes extra time. If you gamble and continue sewing on the same side, it is harder to be accurate and you may find you have to rip that section out, which is the more annoying of the two options.

## Dealing with Intersections

When an existing seam must be crossed by a new line of stitching, the old seam will already be pressed to one side or the other, and it should just be stitched right over, disturbing it as little as possible. When the existing seam comes into the new seam at a sharp angle, care must be taken that the seam allowance is smoothed down, and that there is no excess fullness in the fabric underneath, or the point will be distorted on the front of the work. If there is a small amount of distortion, it can sometimes be eased by clipping into the seam allowance on the back to free it, but a great deal of distortion will require that the seam be redone.

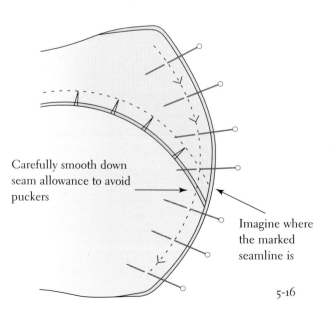

Carefully smooth down seam allowance to avoid puckers

Imagine where the marked seamline is

5-16

There is also a short distance where you will not be able to see the marked line, because it is under the seam allowance. The best thing to do is to lift up the seam allowance and take a peek at it before you actually get there, so you know generally where the line is. Then aim for the next section of mark that you can see and try to keep the curve smooth.

Occasionally, when the seam allowance of an existing seam has been pressed away from the new seam, a small gap in the seam allowance may occur, which can be unnerving. Just stitch the new seam accurately on the line, and the gap should remain completely in the seam allowance and not be a problem (5-17).

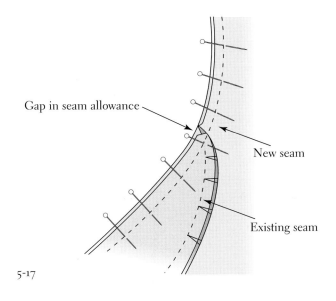

Gap in seam allowance

New seam

Existing seam

5-17

After a seam is finished, you may be dismayed to discover that, in spite of careful pinning and sewing, you have missed the sewing line on the underside by a fair margin. Before you panic, check to see if the seam is a smooth curve. Then flip it over and see how it looks on the front. The fact that all the curves are on the bias provides a generous margin for error. If it looks as if it will lay flat after clipping and pressing, you can probably leave it. However, if you have missed by so much that there will be extra fabric that can't be pressed out on one side of the seam, that small section should be redone. Don't rip the whole seam, just the section that needs correction. Small inaccuracies won't do much harm, but if inaccuracies are significant, and there are a great many of them, the whole piece could be distorted. After you have

done a little curved seam sewing, you will be able to judge fairly easily which seams needs to be redone, but in the beginning, be very conservative in your judgments.

## Secrets to Success
### Clip! Clip! Clip!

The next step is to clip the curves, and *every* curved seam needs clipping. The clipping is done perpendicular to the stitching and needs to go right down to the seamline if it is to do any good at all. Clip every inch for a gradual curve, every half inch for a sharp curve, and even more if necessary. Even the seams that don't look like they need it benefit from clipping, because it relaxes the seam, giving it the flex and stretch that curves require. Obviously, clipping needs to be done carefully, with a pair of scissors that are sharp right to the tip, and care should be taken not to clip the seam itself. In addition, loosely woven fabrics should be clipped very cautiously so that the fabric doesn't ravel down close to the seam.

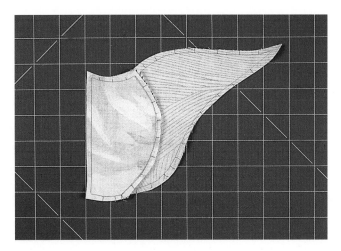

5-18  Clipping allows curved seam to lie flat

## Press! Press! Press!

In addition to clipping, every seam (even those stitched by hand) needs to be pressed individually in order to determine whether it will lie flat. If it doesn't, the situation needs to be corrected now, not four steps down the road. Errors and inaccuracies multiply very quickly with curved seams, so each step needs to be checked carefully before proceeding with the next.

I press with lots of steam and determination. Pressing can do wonders for a seam that doesn't look quite perfect. Even small puckers can be eliminated with the use of a little steam, but it is important to press with an up and down motion, not a side-to-side, scrubbing motion, so as to avoid stretching any of the bias edges or seams.

The seam allowances should both be pressed to one side, and the proper side is determined by the aesthetics of the design. Pressing seam allowances to one side of a seam adds two layers of fabric to that side, creating more bulk. The added bulk gives the impression that this piece of fabric is on top of, or in front of, the adjacent piece. Frequently that is exactly the impression that is needed. For instance, the bird in 5-19 has been improperly pressed and it looks as though it is sinking into the background. The bird in 5-20 looks like it is on top of the background area, because all seams have been pressed inward toward the bird.

5-20   Properly pressed

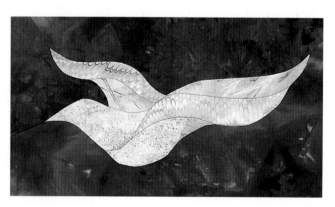

5-19   Improperly pressed

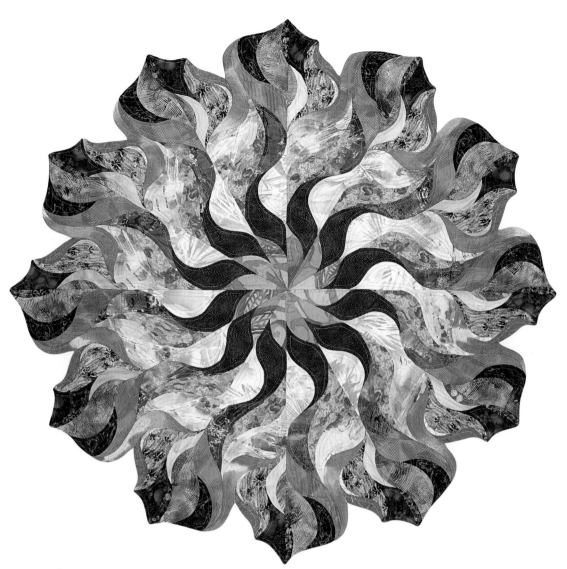

BUDS, 1995
52" diameter, *Judy B. Dales. Quilted by Cindy Williams*

Thinking that the number of pieces in my previous Kaleidomosaic quilts would intimidate other quilters who might be considering trying this style, I thought it might be prudent to create one that had fewer pieces. This particular design has only seventeen pieces in each wedge, which is a good deal easier to manage than some of my other designs. Obviously, the number of pieces, and their size, dictate that this quilt be a bit smaller also.

If you encounter seams where there is no aesthetic reason for pressing a certain way, press whichever way the fabric tends to want to go, but be consistent with subsequent seams. Occasionally one fabric will be heavier, or stronger than its neighbors, in which case, I let the seam lie whichever way it prefers. Press from the back first, so that you can coax the seam allowance to the proper side, then press the front. Take care to eliminate any fold-overs (places on the front where one side tends to roll over the seam), and press out any puckers or excess fullness. If these problems can't be eliminated with a good pressing, the seam will need to be redone to correct the situation.

## Extra Sewing Tips

It is important to keep your work neat, which means keeping seam allowances neat and tidy, cutting all excess threads, and pressing carefully as you go along. Even though it is annoying to have to do so, I am meticulous about cutting all threads off of every piece as I finish a seam. I have discovered that if I leave a bunch of dangling threads, my work begins to look messy, and if the work looks messy, my sewing tends to get sloppy. So I try to keep things as neat as possible to counter this tendency, and I am pleased if the back of the work (5-22) looks as tidy as the front (5-21).

Curves are incredibly forgiving, as you will discover. Seams that look hopelessly inaccurate will actually press out quite flat, and this is due to the fact that most of the edges are bias. However, this also means that the cut pieces have to be handled very carefully. In all my years of quilting, I have never really had any problems with fabric stretching, and I think this is due to the fact that I handle fabric with great respect. I don't yank it around, but treat it gently, and it rewards me by behaving well. I very rarely finger press, because I feel that this might stretch the seam, and if I have to "undo" a seam, I pick the stitches out carefully, rather than ripping or yanking them out, which could distort the fabric. In fact, if I have to take a seam out more than twice, I generally cut an entirely new piece of fabric because that much handling usually creates a mess.

5-21   Front

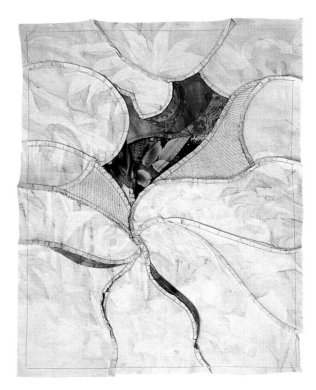

5-22   Back

## Perfect Points

One of the delightful things you will discover as you piece curves is that long, sharp points look very impressive, but are really quite simple. In traditional patchwork, a number of points generally come together at one specific place, which is what makes them so difficult. With curved piecing, however, you often get a single, sharp point where one seam melds into another. If the sewing of both seams is done carefully and accurately, right on the pencil line, the sharp point simply happens on its own and will be there in all its glory when you turn the work to the front. When you encounter a sharp point in appliqué work, it can be very frustrating and time-consuming to convince all the excess fabric to stay tucked neatly under the tip. In piecing, all that excess fabric ends up on the back, as seam allowance, and creates absolutely no problem! It's almost magical and one of the advantages of piecing curves that we can all appreciate.

My quilt *Studio View* on pages 63 and 66 is full of long, skinny points, which look very impressive, but were really very easy to piece, as were the ones on the little demo quilt. Notice that the seam allowances can be either pressed to one side, or both pressed inward, which takes determination but creates the impression that the skinny piece is lying on top of the background.

5-23 Front

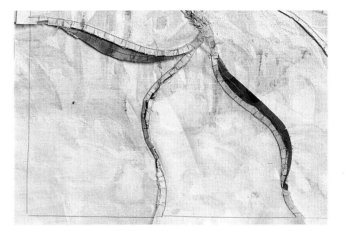

5-24 Back

If you do have a large number of points coming into the center of a quilt, such as is often the case with Curved Kaleidomosaic designs, sew the two halves separately, then join them. When stitching to the point, be careful to end the row of stitching as accurately as possible, stopping precisely at the end of the marked sewing line (not the edge of the fabric), as shown in 5-25. When you have both halves stitched, join them, but don't stitch across the intersection. Sew one half of the seam, then backstitch and end the line of stitching when you reach the intersection. Begin again on the other side of the intersection, taking care not to catch any seam allowances, and finish sewing the seam. This method avoids sewing across the intersection, which is always a problem because of the excessive bulk. When you are finished, you will have a number of accurate points, but there will almost invariably be a hole in the very center (5-26). Eliminate this hole by running a thread through the seam allowance on the back (at the very tip of the points). Anchor the thread securely at the beginning, and draw it up tightly as you work your way completely around to the beginning again. It's sort of like tightening a drawstring purse, and works on the same principle. When the thread is tight and the hole closed, anchor the thread. You should have a very tidy intersection with beautifully sharp points (5-27), and if the seam allowances are all pressed in the same direction, the bulk will be evenly distributed.

Occasionally, you might encounter a curve that looks impossible, and if it looks impossible, it just may be! I see no reason why such a curve couldn't be appliquéd instead of pieced. In fact, sometimes you can piece one portion of a seam and appliqué the one small section that is troublesome. If you press the seam consistently, there should be no visible difference on the front of the work when the quilt is finished.

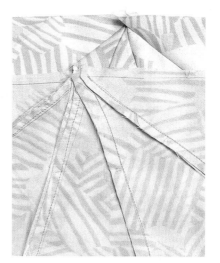

5-25  Front and back view of both halves

5-26  Hole formed at intersection

5-27  Hole eliminated

Chapter Six
# Finishing

Mellow Yellow, 1986
56" x 64", *Judy B. Dales*

This is the third in a series of wave quilts, and I finally figured out how to make them look three dimensional.

# Getting It Straight
## Squaring Up the Quilt

When the pieced portion of your quilt top is finished, it may need to be squared up. Measure the top at several different points through the center sections of the quilt to determine if it is square or not. If not, a small amount of distortion may be eliminated by one final good pressing and a little more clipping. If even just a few seams have not been clipped enough to relax them, this can be enough to pull the whole top out of alignment. If after more clipping it is still distorted, you may have to trim the edges. With a curved design, there are usually no obvious straight lines to be concerned with, so you can often trim one or two sides without producing any harmful, visual effects.

## Borders

The addition of borders may help to correct any distortion in the top. Measure the top accurately through the middle of the quilt, and then cut the borders to the exact measurement. Cutting the borders exactly will ensure that excess fullness on any given side of the quilt will be eased and eliminated when the borders are added. Many a quilter has been known to simply cut a border piece without measuring, and sew it on, but this method will exacerbate any rippling effects present on the edges. Be sure to use the center measurement, not the one from the edges, as the two measurements may not be the same, and the edge measurement is generally less accurate.

The decision to add borders or not is a purely personal one. Many of my free-form curved designs are framed only with a dark binding, which I think enhances the contemporary look. If a border is added, it is imperative that it be well integrated with the main design, carrying over either color, shapes, or specific fabrics. The width of the border must be carefully calculated so that the border frames, but does not overwhelm, the pieced design. Remember that a border's sole purpose is to enhance and frame the piece, not provide extra space to show off your quilting, display piecing skills, or include something extra that just doesn't fit in the main body of the quilt!

## One Final Check

Check one last time to ensure that all dangling threads are snipped, all seams are clipped and neatly trimmed, and seam allowances are pressed in the proper direction. A little care at this point will make the quilting process easier and is well worth the effort. Give the top one final pressing, both front and back.

# Quilting

The quilting design for a curved seam quilt needs to have the same kind of fluid look and grace as the pieced design. Generally, the most effective pattern is one that follows the pieced design, but background areas will often need something more elaborate. I generally do not mark a quilting pattern, but simply let my needle wander where it may. If you are in doubt as to what kind of a quilting design would be appropriate, use tracing paper over your original small drawing and experiment with different patterns.

Baste the quilt thoroughly with whichever method you prefer (thread, pins, or a tacking machine), smoothing all three layers carefully to eliminate creases or puckers. The type of batting you choose is important to the finished look of the quilt and your choice should be based on thorough research. Harriet Hargrave offers excellent information about different battings in her book *From Fiber To Fabric* and offers very specific instructions for testing different batts. Some are excellent for machine quilting because the batt seems to grab the fabric layers and discourages slipping. When I quilt by hand, however, I look for a thin batt that will needle well. Since I use a lot of heavier weight decorator fabrics, I use the thinnest batt I can find in order to cut down on the thickness through which I will be stitching.

The choice of thread for quilting is a personal one, and it too should be based on research and personal experience. I avoid using a starkly contrasting color if I think I will have trouble quilting a certain piece, because the contrast will accentuate any problems with the stitches. I have recently begun experimenting with all sorts of exotic threads (metallic, iridescent, rayon, silk) for machine quilting, but remain pretty traditional when it comes to thread for hand quilting.

SOW IN TEARS, REAP IN JOY, 1993
49" x 59", *Judy B. Dales*

This quilt is the third in the series of three quilts that I made after my mother died.
I intended for the quilt to be a celebration of life, so I chose bright, joyful colors and
had images of fire and water in mind when drawing the design. The quilt was originally
intended to hang horizontally, but I was enchanted with the dancing figure that emerged
when the quilt was turned the other direction and decided it should hang that way.
The title refers to the idea that the passage of time renders the pain of loss less severe,
and as the time for grieving passes, one needs to return to the full joy of living.

Choosing a wonderful print for the back of the quilt is a reward I allow myself after finishing the top! I back my quilts with something colorful because a busy print stands up to the rigors of travel, and I enjoy seeing it each time I fold and pack the quilt. It is a challenge to find just the right print to compliment the front of the quilt, and occasionally I have been able to use a favorite fabric that never worked quite right in the front design of a quilt.

# Finishing
## Binding

The binding for your quilt can be any kind you prefer, but I generally use bias binding, which is made from strips cut diagonally across the fabric, rather than along the length or width. Bias binding is a bit elastic and can be stretched ever so slightly as it is applied. This can help eliminate any rippling or wavering on the edge of the quilt. However, take care not to stretch the binding too much or it will make the center of the quilt billow.

If you need to bind an irregular edge, a thin bias binding works fine if the points on the edge are not too sharp nor the concave angles too deep. The stretch of the bias should also allow the binding to go smoothly around curves, both concave and convex.

Applying binding to an irregular edge

When applying binding by hand to an irregular edge, angles requiring tucks and sharp points need a miter. The binding is stitched on with a ¼" seam,

right sides together. At the concave angle, stitch to the exact middle of the angle and secure the end of stitching with several backstitches. Fold the binding so that it will align properly with the next segment of edge to be stitched, which will cause the binding to form a pleat at the angle. Slip your needle through the bottom of the pleat and begin the next section of stitching with a backstitch as close as possible to where the previous stitching ended. When the binding is turned to the back, this pleat is used to incorporate excess fabric at the angle. Tuck the extra in carefully, and stitch down the fold.

The sharp point is treated in much the same manner, and the miter is similar to the one you would use on a 90° angle. Stitch into the point, ending the row of stitching with several backstitches in the exact middle of the point (¼" away from all edges). Form a pleat in the binding at the tip, which will allow the binding to line up with the next segment of edge. Slip your needle through the bottom of the pleat, and begin the next section of stitching with a backstitch at a point as close as possible to where you ended the last stitching. Notice that the top fold of the pleat does not line up with the edge of the quilt, as it does with a 90° miter, because the angle is different. When the binding is turned to the back, a nice sharp miter will be formed, which should be stitched closed on the front and back.

## Facing

If you feel applying binding is too difficult, you can turn the raw edge of the top and back in toward each other and blind stitch them together, which is called a knife edge. However, I don't think these types of edges look very tidy, so I recommend a facing. The procedure is similar to making a pillow in which you stitch two pieces of fabric right sides together, then turn them right sides out, which creates a finished edge.

When buying fabric for the back of the quilt, buy double the amount needed. The basting and quilting are done in the normal manner using half the backing fabric, and after the quilting is finished, the batting and backing are trimmed even with the outer edge of the top. Place the second piece of backing fabric on a

THINKING BREEZY THOUGHTS, 1997
29" x 29", *Judy B. Dales*

This block was designed by Margaret Fergus of Spring, Texas, in one of my classes,
and she was kind enough to give me permission to use it. The block, which generates
a wonderful feeling of movement, has enough detail that it worked nicely as the
center of a small medallion-style wallhanging.

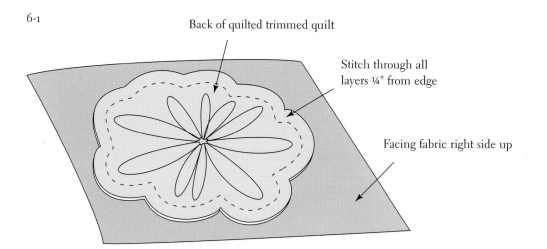

Back of quilted trimmed quilt

Stitch through all layers ¼" from edge

Facing fabric right side up

flat surface, right side up, and lay the front of the quilt onto it. With right sides together, stitch around the outer edge ¼" from the raw edge. Trim the seam allowance at the points down as close as you dare, to allow for turning the point, and trim away any excess batting. Clip into any concave angles and concave curves.

You now have what looks like an inside-out pillow case, except that there is no opening for turning it right side out. To create an opening, cut the whole center of the facing fabric away. Pinch a piece of the fabric about 2" away from the edge, and pull it up and away from the quilt in order to make a little slit into which the scissors can be inserted. Trim the facing to create a 2"-wide band (or any other width you prefer) all the way around. The whole center is still intact, so that large hunk of fabric gets carefully folded and put back into your stash so it isn't wasted.

Turn the facing to the back, using a knitting needle or wooden skewer to turn the sharp points. Pull even more of the batting out of the points if you have difficulty getting them to turn. When the facing is turned to the back, pin it in place with the raw edge turned under ¼", and blind stitch to the back of the quilt, being careful that the stitches don't go all the way through to the front. Because the facing and backing are the same fabric, the facing will be almost invisible, as shown on the following page on the back of *Buds*.

Cut center away leaving 2"-wide facing

Turn facing to quilt back and pin in place

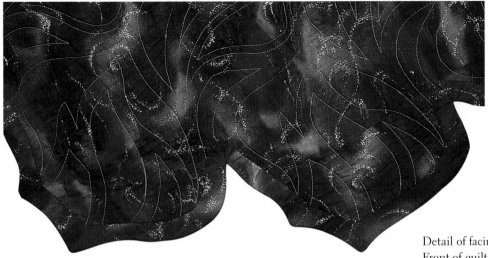

Detail of facing on the back of *Buds*.
Front of quilt shown on page 115.

## Hanging Mechanisms

If you intend to display your quilt on a wall, you will
need a method of hanging it. For a square or rectangular quilt, sew a double sleeve (one made from
a complete tube of fabric) to the back of the quilt at
the top, taking care that the stitches don't go through
to the front. I like to have a break in the middle of the
sleeve so that when I run a flat wooden board (treated
with wood sealer) through the sleeve, there can be
a hanging hook in the middle. I use a staple gun
to create a hook out of monofilament line (heavy
duty fishing line), and then the quilt can hang from
a single hook, just as a picture might.

6-2

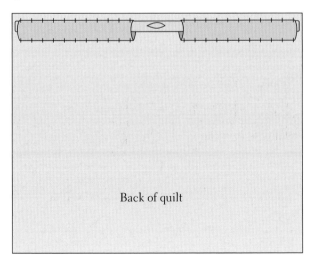

Back of quilt

6-3

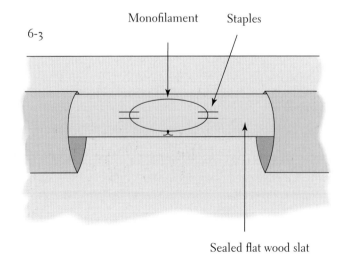

Monofilament    Staples

Sealed flat wood slat

For irregularly shaped quilts, I attach a hanging mechanism at the top edge of the quilt and then apply "stretchers pieces" at strategic places lower down to prevent the edges from flopping in. The hanging mechanism is a flat piece of wood about 4" long that is sealed with wood sealer and completely encased in a fabric casing. This is stitched to the back of the quilt and has a monofilament loop attached to it using a staple gun. The whole weight of the quilt hangs from this loop. The "stretcher pieces" are simply wooden slats that I apply to the back of the quilt with Velcro®. For example, a circular quilt would have a hanger at the top, and two stretchers, one across the widest, middle part of the quilt, and another halfway between those two, about one quarter of the way down the circle. This method works very well for all sorts of odd-shaped quilts.

An even simpler hanging method is to attach the quilt to the wall with Velcro dots all along the top edge and sides. Sew small pieces of Velcro to fabric and sew these to the back of the quilt. Staple gun the other half of the Velcro to the wall. The weight should be evenly distributed to all of the Velcro dots, and there should be enough of them to bear the weight. Carefully peel the two pieces of Velcro apart when removing the quilt from the wall, as the Velcro can quite easily be pulled right off of the wall if you tug on the quilt to get it down.

To ensure that an irregularly shaped quilt will hang properly and look its best when sent to a quilt show, I baste it to a curtain (check to see if they prefer a dark or light color). A sleeve at the top of the curtain makes my irregularly shaped quilt as easy to hang as all the others.

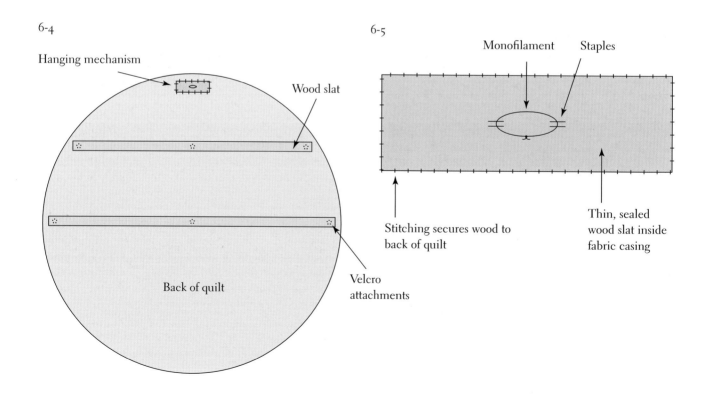

6-4

Hanging mechanism

Wood slat

Back of quilt

Velcro attachments

6-5

Monofilament          Staples

Stitching secures wood to back of quilt

Thin, sealed wood slat inside fabric casing

## Postscript

After quilting for so many years, I was astounded when I finally discovered curved-seam patchwork! Why did it take me so long? Adding curves to my designs allowed me to explore a whole new type of design and to produce quilts that I feel express me, and my personality, so much better than straight line patterns. When I begin to mourn the wasted years spent doing other things, I must remind myself that it was all part of the journey, and I might not be here, in this creative place, right now, if I had not traveled the exact path that I did.

It is my hope that by sharing what I have learned about curves, I can speed you along on your creative journey. I trust that the information in this book will open many doors for you, allowing you to produce the quilts that you were destined to create. Sewing curves definitely takes more effort, but I feel the splendid results are more than worth the effort. A quilter can never have too many different techniques to choose from, nor ideas from which to choose. Hopefully, learning how to draw, design with, and piece curves will enable you to translate what is in your heart into your quilts. Enjoy!

LIBERATED LANDSCAPE II, 1997
57" x 48", *Judy B. Dales*

This is the second in a series of fragmented landscapes. In this piece, the original landscape was pieced, then embellished with appliquéd details. After it is segmented, random pieced strips are inserted to give the quilt an impressionistic feel.

Chapter Seven

# The Gallery

I have been teaching curved-seam techniques for a number of years, and in this section, you will find some of my students' work. Notice that often it is the more simple designs that make the most effective quilts, proving once again that designs do not have to be complex to be wonderful. It is usually the student who is most realistic when assessing her skills, motivation, and perseverance who will have the most success. All of the designs shown here are the students' own, which I hope will inspire you to try your hand at drawing curves also. You will discover, as they did, that it is easier than you think!

BEAD DAZZLED FIREBALL, 1994
40" x 50", *Mary Nehring*, Versailles, KY

Mary created a Kaleidoscope motif, but she appliquéd the curved-seam section onto a banner-style wallhanging. It is unusual for the pointed edge to be at the top, but it is unique and quite charming. The dark, rich purple of the background intensifies the colors of the curved pieces, and the beads give the whole piece a bit of sparkle.

Fuchsia Fantasy, work in progress
54" diameter, *Deb Lybarger*, Akron, OH

Deb spent almost two years searching for just the right fabrics for this wallhanging.
Yellow is Deb's favorite color, so it was a natural choice for this fuchsia flower design,
but as she discovered, it has to be used with care. The yellow on the outer rim of her
quilt balances the strong yellows in the center, evokes the bright sunlight of a summer
garden, and gives her piece the perfect finishing touch.

FANTASIA, 1995
54" diameter, *JoAnn (Jodee) Todd*, Rochester, NY

Jodee's Kaleidomosaic design looks very three dimensional, and her curves are full of
motion! Notice the soft, muted background fabrics she has used, which add so much to
the overall look of the quilt.

VERMONT DANCE, 1992
26" x 30", *JoAnn (Jodee) Todd*, Rochester, NY

Jodee is one of the speediest quilters I know, but she sacrifices nothing for that speed. Her curved seams are flawless, the designs spectacular, and best of all, her quilts get finished! Jodee started this during a class at Quilt Inn, my yearly seminar in Vermont, using cut paper shapes, and then was inspired to finish it by drawing freehand.

Other Curved Things, 1997
21" x 24", *Lisa Sharpe*, Cranbrook, B.C., Canada

My class on curved-seam piecing is called "Waves, Wings, and Other Curved Things," and since Lisa's piece is definitely not wings, or waves, the title is very appropriate! Because the figures created by free form curves are not realistic, they provide a wonderful opportunity to experiment with colors, values, and textures. The fabrics Lisa chose heighten the feeling of fantasy, but at the same time, give you the feeling that you might like to live in a place where such a flower would grow. Lisa's design was created using the cut-paper exercise.

**BIRDS FROM CEDAR LAKES**, 1995
35" x 30", *Peggy Stocks*, Manson, NC

Peggy used three of the birds from my curved-seam class and made a lovely wallhanging. Even though this bird looks charmingly simple, it contains all of the challenges inherent in curved-seam piecing, and anyone who gets one together can feel justifiably proud. Peggy did three! Bravo!

**JULIE'S FISH QUILT**, 1993
48" x 36", *Pat Crucil*, Sechelt, B.C., Canada

This quilt has perfectly captured the undulating motion of the ocean and the lackadaisical life of the fish who call it home. Just looking at it transports me to quiet, soothing places. The fabrics are hand-dyed and marbleized, and actual fish were used to stamp the ink onto the fabric, which is an ancient Japanese method of stamping called *gymotaku*.

WATERLILY 1993
31" x 31", *Priscilla Evans Hair*, Easley, SC

The beautiful hand quilting on this piece enhances the curves in Priscilla's graceful flower. Curves lend themselves to suggesting, but not quite replicating, the forms of nature, so each viewer can derive her own interpretation from a design. This one is clearly a flower, and a beautiful one, at that.

JUDY'S STARS FOR MARY'S KITCHEN, 1994
27" x 35", *Mary Smith*, New Providence, NJ

The colors in Mary's quilt were chosen to coordinate with the colors in her kitchen, which is where this piece proudly hangs. The swooping curves give the irregular stars a wonderful feeling of motion.

WILD FLOWER, 1995
58" diameter, *Mildred Dort*, Dunedin, FL

Mildred's Kaleidomosaic design has just enough asymmetry in the wedge to give each section of the flower a little twirl, and her choice of colors has produced a wonderfully soothing quilt. Photo: *Mildred Dort*

Pure Ecstasy a.k.a. Come Again, 1997
22½" x 25½", *Vicki L. Ibison*, Kalispell, MT

I won't even begin to interpret the title of this quilt for you. Better, I think, to leave it to your imagination, but the design certainly suggests something intense, vibrant, and exciting! Notice how the heavily quilted background and a little trapunto encourages the figure to float above the surface, and also how the lines in the background continually draw your eye back to the center of the design.

It's a Black-Tie Affair, 1997
33" x 43", *Darcy Young*, Houston, TX

Although she has been an accomplished seamstress for years, Darcy took up quilting less than a year before she created this quilt. The design is one I created using the cut-paper design exercise, and Darcy interpreted it in sophisticated black, gray, and white fabric to create a very elegant look. The beautiful machine quilting enhances the curved lines, and extending the curves into the border area adds interest and helps to integrate the border with the central part of the quilt. Photo: *Gary Bankhead*

Down Under, 1994
42" x 38", *Mildred Dort*, Dunedin, FL

The curves in this underwater scene evoke the gentle rocking
motion of the water that makes the beautiful vegetation dance
and sway. Collection of *Dorothy Sisko*. Photo: *Mildred Dort*

CONVERSATIONS, 1996
47½" x 48½", *Lois Griffin*, Woodbridge, NJ

Many of the fabrics in this vibrant piece were hand dyed or hand painted by the artist.
Lois is one of the many quilters who has discovered that curves are not really that
difficult to piece. This is Lois's first design with pieced curves, and she very wisely
kept them gentle, but they are effective, nonetheless, and add a bit of softness to the
design. This piece is dedicated to the memory of her cousin, Art Kropp.

ALTAR SERIES, 1997
*Judy B. Dales*

I feel that curves lend themselves very effectively to ecclesiastical work because the softness of the curves can create an ethereal effect. All of the pieces here were done for the United Church of Christ in Mountain Lakes, New Jersey, in 1997. The altar cloth remains on the altar for most of the year, but the four sets of pulpit and lectern hangings are changed so that the colors coincide with the appropriate church season. Here you see the green hangings, which are for general, non-special days in the church calendar. The green hangings are the only set where the two pieces aren't perfectly symmetrical because the Greek letters could not be reversed. Only a few of the curves at the bottom needed to be changed, and I doubt if most people even notice the difference.

The altar cloth was created from a variety of white and "almost white" fabrics because I wanted it to be fairly neutral in color. I was acutely aware, all during the process of making these hangings, that not only would they be in a sacred place, which is intimidating enough, but also that the people looking at them would be, quite literally, a captive audience. Therefore, I wanted them to be very special. About halfway through the process, I started to have anxiety attacks about whether the congregation would like them, because they are very different from the usual church hangings. When I expressed my fears to one of the committee members in charge of acquiring new hangings, she calmed my fears by assuring me that they knew I would create something different, and that is exactly why they asked me to take on the project.

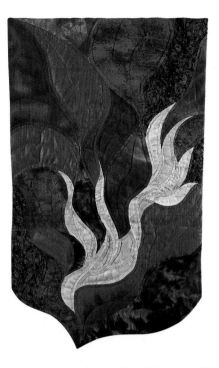

The red hangings are used during the celebration of Pentecost and incorporate both the dove, which symbolizes the descending spirit, and flames, which stand for purification.

Purple is the color used during Advent and Lent, both times of anticipation in the church. The cross and the flame are both common religious symbols, and the two are combined here to produce a transparent, layered effect.

White is the color that stands for purity and is used for many church celebrations. Here again, I've used a cross and combined it with a modernistic star.

My first experience with ecclesiastical textiles was when I decided to make a stole for Dr. Larry Kalp when he was installed as the minister at my church. I was uncertain about which symbols would be appropriate, so I consulted with Larry. The resulting stole has a star, a cross, a dove, water, and a chalice, so it is appropriate for many church occasions.

Chapter Eight

# Projects

## Choosing a Design

In this chapter you will find several patterns. The difficulty of each one has been noted, so if you are very timid about trying curves, choose one of the easier designs. Some of them have been "test driven" by friends who have never sewn curved seams before. In most cases, I gave them the pattern and the text from this book (no illustrations) and they managed to figure everything out. I'm sure you can too.

The patterns are presented on an 8½" x 11" page, so some will need to be enlarged. I have suggested an appropriate size, but feel free to enlarge the design to any size you like, using any of the enlargement methods covered in Chapter Three (pages 74-78).

In most cases, I have not provided specific fabric requirements because these designs should be approached with a spirit of adventure, and I feel it would be a shame for me to select fabric combinations for you. It is my hope that you would choose a different fabric for each piece, making the design process more fun and adventurous.

I am also assuming that many of you have already acquired quite a stash of fabric, and that you can take advantage of that when trying one of these designs. If, however, you feel you need to buy fabric, or need to calculate how much will be needed of any individual fabric, you can make some reasonable estimates after the pattern has been enlarged.

Take a look at the overall dimensions of the piece. If you plan to use the same fabric in all the background areas, you will need a piece of fabric that is at least as big as the quilt itself with a little extra included for seam allowances. For instance, if your quilt will be 24" x 36", a yard of fabric would be more than enough for the background. As you lay out the pieces, lay them down in the order that they will be in the quilt, so that curves align with curves and you don't waste more fabric than necessary.

For the smaller pieces, the only concern would be that you have the length needed for long skinny pieces. A fat quarter of fabric is approximately 18" x 22", so if you have a template that is 26" long, the fat quarter wouldn't be enough, unless you lay the template running diagonally on the fabric.

For the most part, common sense will guide you in determining how much fabric is required. Remember that it is often when our first choice of fabrics doesn't work for whatever reason (such as the amount is not sufficient), that we get very creative. I always buy more than I think I will need, so that I have a bit left over, and you might wish to do the same.

Remember that there is no seam allowance added to any of the templates in the patterns, and that you will be marking the sewing line on the back of the fabric. Trace the pattern, then glue the front of the tracing paper to poster board, so the marks will be on the back of the template. When I first started using this template method, I took to writing key phrases on the templates to help me remember this. One of my favorites is "Front side down, Dummy!" which I write on the front of the template. This never failed to get my attention!

CIRCLES OF DISCOVERY, 1997
28" x 28", *Laurie Lee Martecchini*, Kingwood, TX

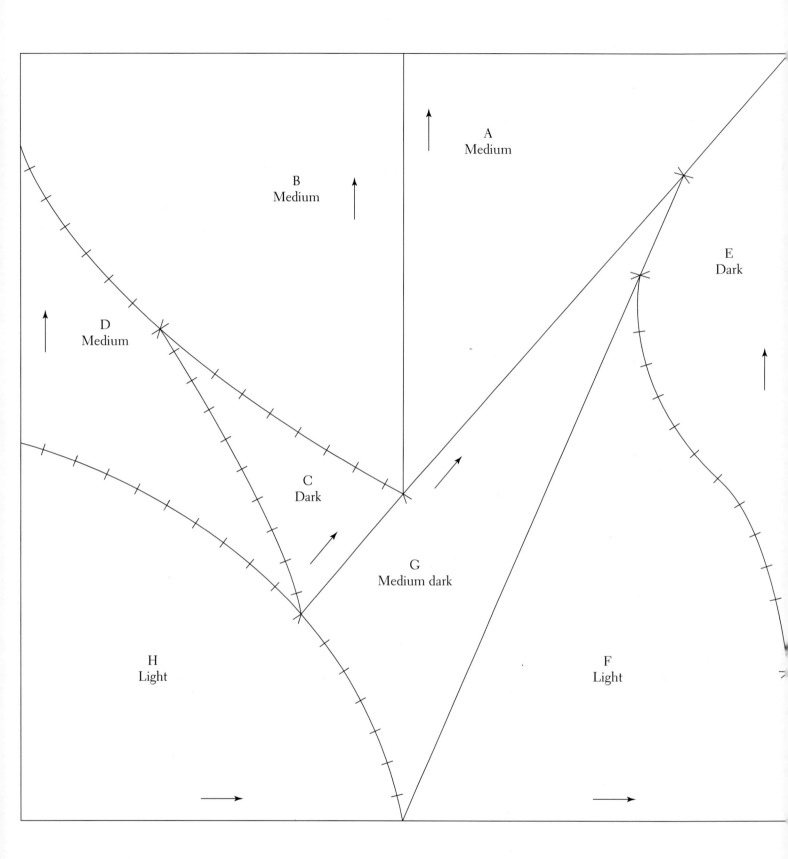

A
Medium

B
Medium

E
Dark

D
Medium

C
Dark

G
Medium dark

H
Light

F
Light

# Circles of Discovery

This small wallhanging consists of four simple blocks rotated around the center point. Laurie worked with 10" blocks, but the ones provided here are 8" blocks. I decided that if I reduced the size to 8", the entire block would fit on the page and there would be no enlargement necessary. The curves in these blocks are not difficult, which would make this project a good one to start with. Laurie is an experienced needlewoman and a meticulous worker, but she has not had much piecing experience. She was absolutely delighted to discover how easy the curves were to sew, and how wonderful they looked when finished and neatly pressed.

Laurie used a light fabric for the background, two very dark fabrics, one medium dark, and three mediums, but you can, of course, play with the design and make other choices. Different parts of the design will dominate, depending on how the colors and values are arranged. A fat quarter of each of the fabrics used is plenty.

Laurie used two different border treatments, a narrow inner border and a wider one to frame the piece. I have changed the measurements slightly from those Laurie used to make the measuring easier. The inner border is 1" wide and overlaps at the corners, so the strips need to be cut 1 ½" wide and 17 ½" long. These can easily be cut from a fat quarter. The outer border is 3" wide, so should be cut 3½" wide by 24½" long. A half yard of fabric would be enough for these borders, but if you have a full yard, you could do the binding out of the same fabric. You will also need a backing fabric at least 25" or 26" (just a little bigger than the top) and batting the same size.

8"
blocks

17"  1" wide
18"
3"
24"

Finished size measurements

## The Eagle

This is one of the designs from my Alaska quilt, shown on page 101. The drawing here is 8¾" x 7" and should be enlarged to at least 20" x 16", and could go even larger if you wish. This is not an easy pattern to sew because there are a lot of pieces, but none of the curves are terribly difficult. If the design is large enough, the pieces should not be too difficult to handle. However, when you are dealing with this number of pieces, great accuracy is required to avoid distortion.

I used assorted feathery prints for the body and wings of the eagle, and a bit of white and yellow for the head, tail feathers, and the beak. The pieces are so small that you can probably work with scrap pieces, but if you intend to purchase fabric, a fat quarter would be more than enough. If you use a swirly, sky-like print for the background, a half yard piece would allow you to choose the exact spot you wish to cut. I appliquéd the eye, which was cut from a solid black print.

My eagle was incorporated into a top with other blocks, but a nice multi-colored border would finish a single block off nicely. A 3" border would be sufficient for the 20" x 16" size eagle block.

THE EAGLE, 1997
20" x 16", *Judy B. Dales*

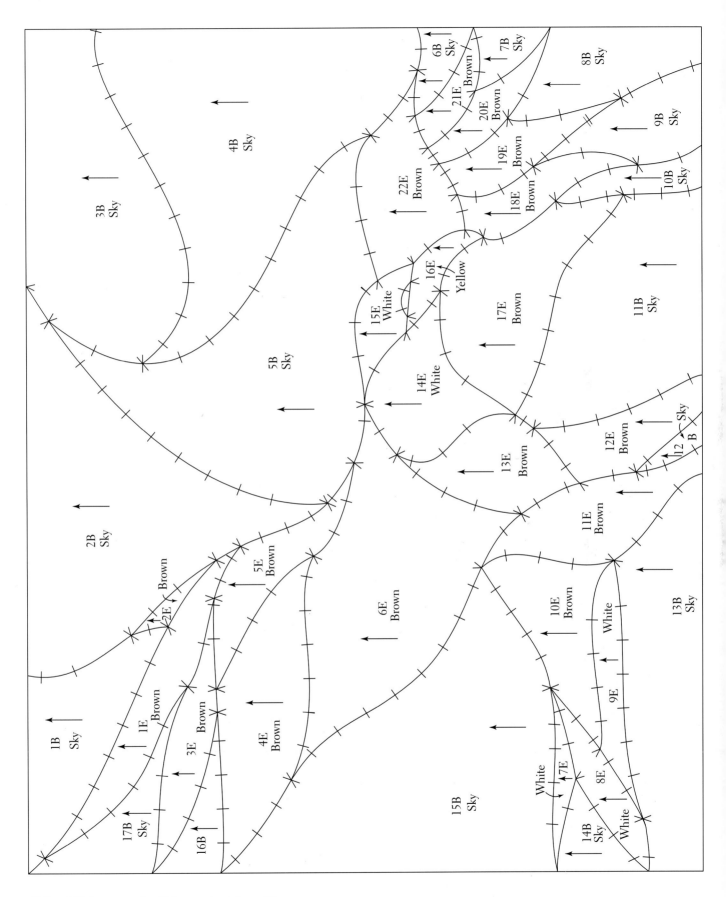

8¾" x 7" Enlarge to 20"x 16" (approximately 229%)

# Practice Petals

This small piece offers a challenge to those of you who wish to try long, skinny curves, or for those who just wish to hone their skills. The curves are relatively gentle, so the piece is not as difficult as you might suspect. The pattern is printed here at half of its proper size, so it needs to be enlarged to 11" x 16", or 200%.

I used a red hand-dyed fabric, a green print, a purple, and one wee bit of yellow. The pieces are very small so they could be cut from assorted scraps. The background requires something light to provide a contrast to the flower form, and I chose a light, airy print. A fat quarter should be enough for the background, but a half yard would allow you to choose where you want to cut and provide a little extra should you have to recut any of the pieces, which are quite large. I used the same green fabric for the border (3½" wide) that was used for the petals. Since the corners are mitered, the length of the border pieces is 23", so you would need either a half yard, or a quarter yard cut across the width of fabric. A fat quarter would not provide the necessary length.

PRACTICE PETALS, 1996
18" x 23", *Judy B. Dales*

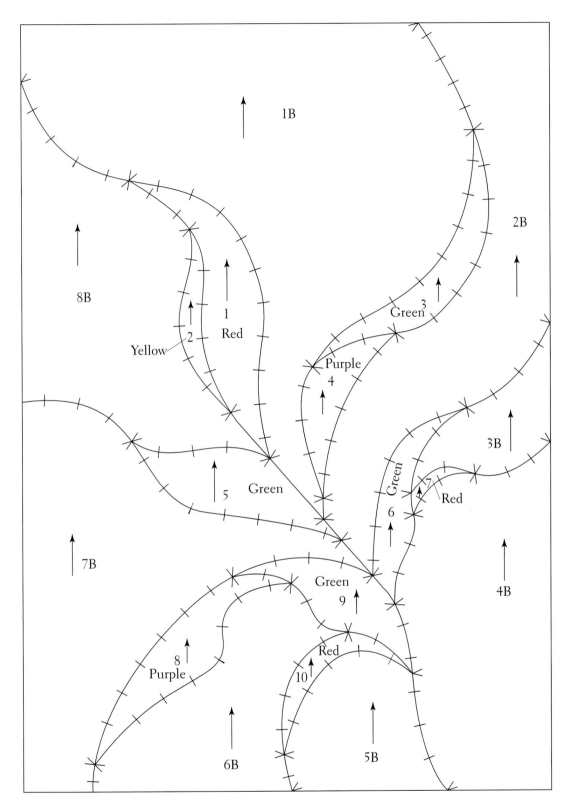

1B

2B

8B

Green 3

1
Red

2

Yellow

Purple
4

8B

Green
5

Green

Green 6

Red

3B

7B

4B

Green
9

Red

Purple
8

10 Red

6B

5B

5 ½" x 8"

# Drifting Along

Kim's wallhanging is composed of fairly simple block units, but the blocks have been placed asymmetrically. If you compare 3-12 on page 68 to the finished quilt, you will see that Kim added some seams to the background areas, which is an option you should also consider. The blocks are 8" square and are given here full size. There are nine complete blocks, which are not terribly difficult to piece, and seven filler blocks, which offer an opportunity for you to draw your own curves. You might also like to photocopy the blocks and create your own arrangement.

Kim used her own hand-dyed and hand-painted fabrics in this design, and took great pleasure in using colors that she knew I would never work with! The fabric placement is the same in all the blocks, but because each part of the texture is unique, it doesn't seem so. Pieces 2 and 7 are cut from the same print

and would require a half yard of fabric. Although Kim has used orange for pieces 1, 4, and 5, they are actually different fabrics. If you use three different fabrics, you will need a fat quarter of each, but if you use the same print for all three pieces, you would need just a half yard. Kim's background looks variegated, but that is due to different coloration in the hand-dyed fabric. It is all the same fabric. You will need a yard of whatever you choose for the background.

If you plan on adding any seamlines to the background blocks, which will make fabric changes necessary, take that into account when figuring yardages. As always, it's a good idea to buy more than you think you actually need. It's nice to have extra if you discover you do need more, and can be used for other projects if you have leftovers.

DRIFTING ALONG, 1997
32" x 32", *Kim Ritter*,
Nassau Bay, TX

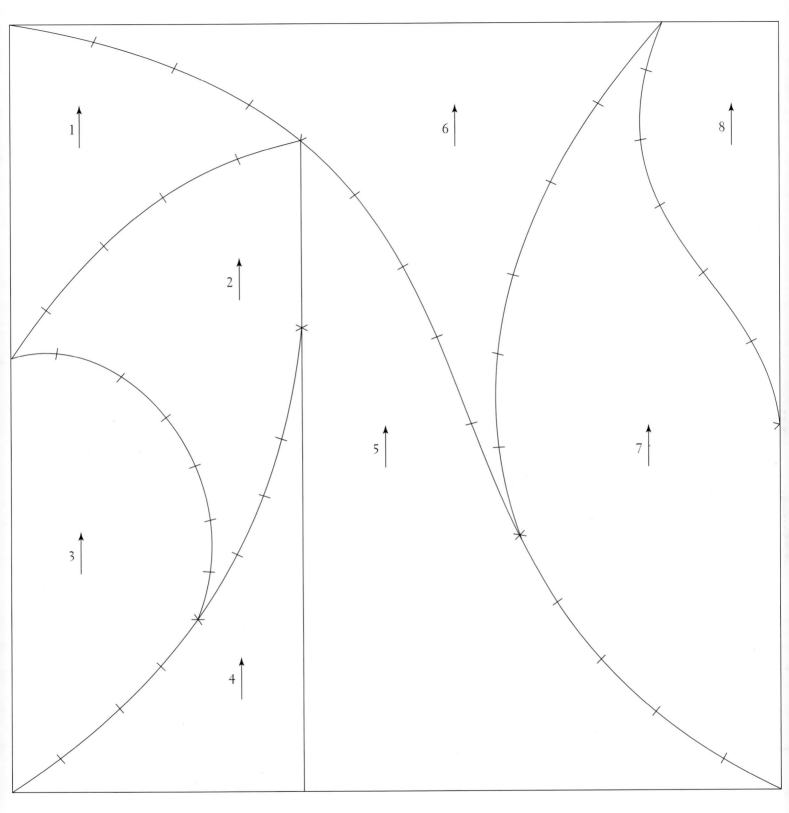

1

2

3

4

5

6

7

8

8" square

# The Bird

This is the design my students use in class to practice their curved-seam piecing, and this little bird has become famous! He looks quite innocuous, but is, in fact, quite a challenge! When I originally designed this pattern, I wanted the project to be small, so that my students would not need much fabric in class, or go home with one more unfinished project. However, I intentionally included all of the problems one would encounter when working with curves, so the students would have experienced all of them. I think of it as the Ph.D. of curved-seam piecing, so if you enjoy a challenge, give this little guy a try!

There are fairly sharp curves in this design, a few S-curves, and lots of places where you have to think ahead to prevent sewing yourself into a corner. Furthermore, many of the pieces look the same backwards and forwards, so care must be taken to keep the pieces in their proper position. One way to ensure that you have a piece positioned properly is to check that the intersection marks are actually where they should be. If they are not, you've got the piece reversed somehow.

I used three fabrics for the bird, and a sky-type fabric for the background. A fat quarter is sufficient for the background, and the bird pieces can probably be cut from odd scraps. I used the same fabric for pieces 5 and 6, because they represent the head and breast of the bird, and I feel they should visually blend. Repeating that same print in piece 3 balances the bird nicely, and I've discovered that it's a good idea to use a multicolored print in these three places.

The fabric for pieces 2 and 7 should be fairly low-key (either dark or dull). These are the more unattractive parts of the bird's anatomy, so you don't want to draw attention to these areas with dynamic colors or exciting textures. The forward part of the wings, however, (pieces 1 and 4) should have an eye-catching fabric, as these are important parts of the design. You may have to experiment with different combinations of fabrics before you find just the right one. Not only is this design tricky to sew, it is also not easy to find just the right combination of fabrics!

The pattern here is three-quarters the size of the original, so you will need to enlarge it to 14" x 8". You could actually go bigger, but be careful not to make the pattern too large, or the bird will look strange. When I reduced the pattern, I had it copied at 75% of the original. In order to return to the original size, you will need to enlarge it by 133%.

A single bird, bordered in a nice print, makes a lovely, small gift, and can usually be sewn in an afternoon. However, don't feel that you must restrict yourself to just one. Peggy Stocks used three in her lovely wallhanging in the quilt on page 133.

THE BIRD, 1990
14" x 20", *Judy B. Dales*

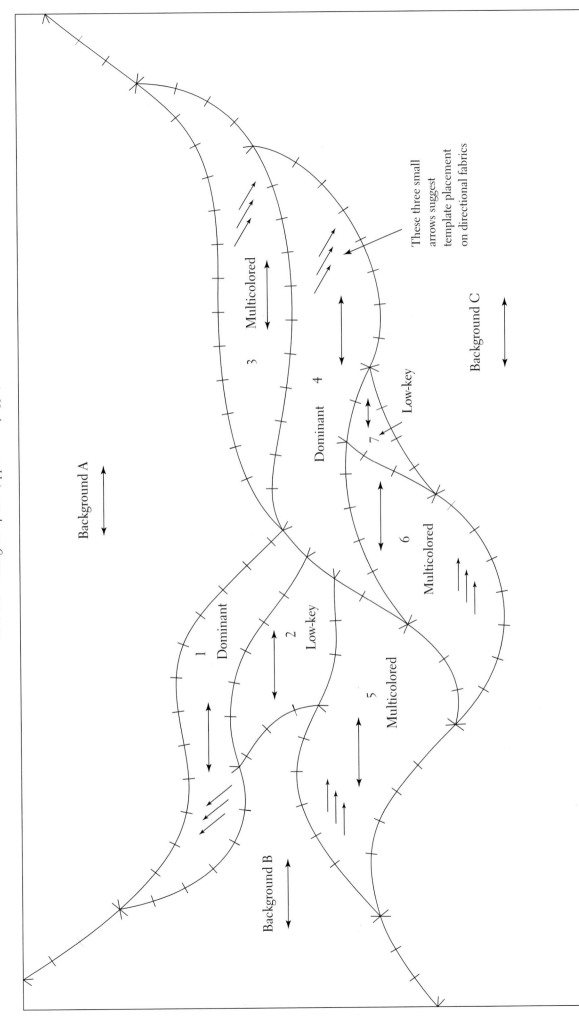

10 ⅜ "x 6 " – Enlarge to 14" x 8" (approximately 133%)

Background A

1 Dominant

3 Multicolored

2 Low-key

Dominant 4

Low-key

7

Background C

These three small arrows suggest template placement on directional fabrics

6 Multicolored

5 Multicolored

Background B

# Bibliography

Bayles, David and Ted Orland. *Art & Fear.* Santa Barbara, CA: Capra Press, 1993.

Beyer, Jinny. *Patchwork Portfolio.* McLean, VA: EPM Publications, Inc., 1989.

Beyer, Jinny. *The Quilter's Album of Blocks & Borders.* McLean, VA: EPM Publications, 1980.

Bourgoin, J. *Design Discovery Coloring Book.* New York, NY: Dover Publications, 1976.

Cornell, Judith. *Drawing the Light from Within.* New York, NY: Prentice Hall Press, 1990.

Critchlow, Keith. *Islamic Patterns, An Analytical and Cosmological Approach.* New York, NY: Schocken Books, 1976.

El-Said, Issam and Ayse Parman. *Geometric Concepts in Islamic Art.* London: World of Islam Festival Publishing Co. Ltd., 1976.

Hargrave, Harriet. *From Fiber to Fabric.* Lafayette, CA: C&T Publishing, 1997.

Meehan, Aidan. *Celtic Design/Spiral Patterns.* London: Thames and Hudson, 1995.

McDowell, Ruth B. *Symmetry, A Design System for Quiltmakers.* Lafayette, CA: C&T Publishing, 1994.

Messent, Jan. *Design Sources for Pattern.* Morecambe, GB: Crochet Design, 1992.

Messent, Jan. *Designing with Motifs and Borders.* Morecambe, GB: Crochet Design, 1995.

Messent, Jan. *Designing with Pattern.* Morecambe, GB: Crochet Design, 1992.

Messent, Jan. *Design Sources for Symbolism.* Morecambe, GB: Crochet Design, 1993.

Schlotzhauer, Joyce. *The Curved Two-Patch System.* McLean, VA: EPM Publications, Inc., 1983.

Schlotzhauer, Joyce. *Curves Unlimited.* McLean, VA: EPM Publications, 1984.

Schlotzhauer, Joyce. *Cutting Up With Curves.* McLean, VA: EPM Publications, Inc., 1988.

DETAIL OF SPIRIT FLIGHT, full view on page 84

# Index

# About the Author

Judy B. Dales began quilting at a time when tradition ruled the quilt world, so she learned to do things the old fashioned way. Today, however, she uses a rotary cutter, experiments with very unusual fabrics, and does the majority of sewing on the machine, but accomplishes other parts of the design process in a fairly traditional manner. She finds the combination of new tools and traditional techniques works well and enables her to translate the designs in her head into fabric.

In the more than a quarter of a century that Judy has been making quilts, she has explored many techniques and design styles, but it was the discovery of curves that truly opened the door to her creativity. She feels great affinity for the curved line, and her work has become more expressive and personal since she began incorporating curves into her quilts. Although the designs require careful preparation, the end result is one of movement, spontaneity, and grace. The fluid nature of the curves creates a feminine look which, along with her unique color palette, makes her work very distinctive.

Judy's other great love is fabric, and her reputation as a superb colorist is firmly established. Her ability to integrate diverse colors and patterns into a soft, subtle union allows the color to flow across the surface, creating a distinctive, painterly effect. Her fabric stash is immense, and she delights in using fabrics that other quilters disdain, creating unique combinations in which the character of the individual fabrics is sublimated to the overall mood she is trying to create.

Many of Judy's quilts have been sold to collectors, corporations, and museums, including *America, The Beautiful*, the New Jersey winner in the first Great American Quilt Contest. Of the numerous awards she has received, two Fellowship Grants from the New Jersey State Council on the Arts are the ones she values most highly. *Spirit Flight*, a quilt made in memory of her mother, is part of the prestigious White House Permanent Craft Collection, has been exhibited at The White House as well as The Smithsonian, and continues to tour with this impressive collection of fine crafts.

Judy earned a teaching certificate in college, but found teaching young children was not to her liking. However, the skills acquired have not been wasted, as Judy spends much of her time teaching color and design to quiltmakers. She is a gifted teacher, bringing to the classroom not only great, good humor and enthusiasm, but also the ability to clarify complicated concepts, encourage the most timid of quilters, and extract amazing levels of creativity from her students. Judy believes that quilting should be fun, and values her teaching experiences for the laughter, energy, and creativity they generate.

Judy and her husband have recently relocated to a suburb of Houston, Texas, after many years in northern New Jersey, but they are looking forward to the time when they can retire to their beloved home state of Vermont. Judy travels extensively to lecture and teach, but the highlight of her teaching calendar every year is the seminar she runs in northern Vermont. For information about the seminar, contact:

**Quilt Inn, Highland Lodge**
**Greensboro, VT 05841**
or contact Judy Dales at:
**6107 Palm Ridge Court**
**Kingwood, TX 77345**

# Other Fine Books From C&T Publishing

An Amish Adventure: 2nd Edition, Roberta Horton

Anatomy of a Doll: The Fabric Sculptor's Handbook, Susanna Oroyan

Appliqué 12 Easy Ways! Elly Sienkiewicz

Art & Inspirations: Ruth B. McDowell, Ruth B. McDowell

The Art of Silk Ribbon Embroidery, Judith Baker Montano

The Artful Ribbon, Candace Kling

Baltimore Beauties and Beyond (Volume I), Elly Sienkiewicz

Basic Seminole Patchwork, Cheryl Greider Bradkin

Beyond the Horizon: Small Landscape Appliqué, Valerie Hearder

Buttonhole Stitch Appliqué, Jean Wells

A Colorful Book, Yvonne Porcella

Colors Changing Hue, Yvonne Porcella

Crazy Quilt Handbook, Judith Montano

Crazy Quilt Odyssey, Judith Montano

Crazy with Cotton, Diana Leone

Deidre Scherer: Work in Fabric & Thread, Deidre Scherer

Dimensional Appliqué: Baskets, Blooms & Baltimore Borders, Elly Sienkiewicz

Easy Pieces: Creative Color Play with Two Simple Blocks, Margaret Miller

Elegant Stitches: An Illustrated Stitch Guide & Source Book of Inspiration, Judith Baker Montano

Enduring Grace: Quilts from the Shelburne Museum Collection, Celia Y. Oliver

Everything Flowers: Quilts from the Garden, Jean and Valori Wells

The Fabric Makes the Quilt, Roberta Horton

Faces & Places: Images in Appliqué, Charlotte Warr Andersen

Fantastic Figures: Ideas & Techniques Using the New Clays, Susanna Oroyan

Focus on Features: Life-like Portrayals in Appliqué, Charlotte Warr Andersen

Forever Yours, Wedding Quilts, Clothing & Keepsakes, Amy Barickman

Fractured Landscape Quilts, Katie Pasquini Masopust

Free Stuff for Quilters on the Internet, Judy Heim and Gloria Hansen

From Fiber to Fabric: The Essential Guide to Quiltmaking Textiles, Harriet Hargrave

Hand Quilting with Alex Anderson: Six Projects for Hand Quilters, Alex Anderson

Heirloom Machine Quilting, Third Edition, Harriet Hargrave

Imagery on Fabric, Second Edition, Jean Ray Laury

Impressionist Palette, Gai Perry

Impressionist Quilts, Gai Perry

Jacobean Rhapsodies: Composing with 28 Appliqué Designs, Patricia B.Campbell and Mimi Ayars

Judith Baker Montano: Art & Inspirations, Judith B. Montano

Kaleidoscopes & Quilts, Paula Nadelstern

Mariner's Compass Quilts, New Directions, Judy Mathieson

Mastering Machine Appliqué, Harriet Hargrave

Michael James: Art & Inspirations, Michael James

The New Sampler Quilt, Diana Leone

On the Surface: Thread Embellishment & Fabric Manipulation, Wendy Hill

Papercuts and Plenty, Vol. III of Baltimore Beauties and Beyond, Elly Sienkiewicz

Patchwork Persuasion: Fascinating Quilts from Traditional Designs, Joen Wolfrom

Patchwork Quilts Made Easy, Jean Wells (co-published with Rodale Press, Inc.)

Pattern Play, Doreen Speckmann

Pieced Clothing Variations, Yvonne Porcella

Pieces of an American Quilt, Patty McCormick

Piecing: Expanding the Basics, Ruth B. McDowell

Plaids & Stripes: The Use of Directional Fabrics in Quilts, Roberta Horton

Quilts for Fabric Lovers, Alex Anderson

Quilts from the Civil War: Nine Projects, Historical Notes, Diary Entries, Barbara Brackman

Quilts, Quilts, and More Quilts! Diana McClun and Laura Nownes

Recollections, Judith Baker Montano

RIVA: If Ya Wanna Look Good Honey, Your Feet Gotta Hurt..., Ruth Reynolds

Say It with Quilts, Diana McClun and Laura Nownes

Scrap Quilts: The Art of Making Do, Roberta Horton

Simply Stars: Quilts that Sparkle, Alex Anderson

Six Color World: Color, Cloth, Quilts & Wearables, Yvonne Porcella

Small Scale Quiltmaking: Precision, Proportion, and Detail, Sally Collins

Soft-Edge Piecing, Jinny Beyer

Start Quilting with Alex Anderson: Six Projects for First-Time Quilters, Alex Anderson

Stripes in Quilts, Mary Mashuta

Tradition with a Twist: Variations on Your Favorite Quilts, Blanche Young and Dalene Young Stone

Trapunto by Machine, Hari Walner

The Visual Dance: Creating Spectacular Quilts, Joen Wolfrom

Wildflowers: Designs for Appliqué & Quilting, Carol Armstrong

Willowood: Further Adventures in Buttonhole Stitch Appliqué, Jean Wells

Yvonne Porcella: Art & Inspirations, Yvonne Porcella

For more information write for a free catalog:
C&T Publishing, Inc.
P.O. Box 1456
Lafayette, CA 94549
(800) 284-1114
http://www.ctpub.com
e-mail: ctinfo@ctpub.com

For quilting supplies:
Cotton Patch Mail Order
3405 Hall Lane, Dept. CTB
Lafayette, CA 94549
e-mail: cottonpa@aol.com
(800) 835-4418
(925) 283-7883